CONTEN

Introduction   7

1. What Is Complex Trauma?   15
2. Where Does C-PTSD Come From?   31
3. Symptoms of PTSD   60
4. Affect Dysregulation   88
5. Negative Self-Concept   111
6. Disturbed Interpersonal Relationships   149
7. Recovering and Reclaiming Your Identity   173

Final Words   203
Notes   207

RECOVERY FROM COMPLEX PTSD

FROM TRAUMA TO REGAINING SELF THROUGH MINDFULNESS & EMOTIONAL REGULATION EXERCISES

DON BARLOW

A ROADTOTRANQUILITY BOOK

NO MORE

START SAYING NO
LEARN TO SAY NO WITHOUT
EXPLAINING YOURSELF

DON BARLOW

Before we get into the book, let me offer you a free mini-book. Scan this QR code to claim your FREE People-Pleasing No More mini-book!

INTRODUCTION

Is your daily life impacted by previous traumatic experiences? Post-Traumatic Stress Disorder (PTSD) is more common than many people believe, with an estimated 3.5% of the population, or approximately eight million Americans, suffering from it (Hull, 2020).[1] Researchers discovered a particularly severe form, known as Complex PTSD, with even more serious consequences.

Do you have difficulty developing and maintaining solid relationships with other people? You may find it very hard to trust anyone other than yourself and to be intimate with them. These interpersonal problems have also very likely affected your sense of self-esteem, which makes you feel worthless or "less-than" the people around you. You're experiencing flashbacks to your painful past and getting trapped in negative thought loops.

Struggling to function in daily life can be incredibly frustrating, especially when others around you seem to be handling the ups and downs just fine. It's not because you are unworthy, or not as smart as other people, or because you lack some kind of ability that everyone else seems to have. Your troubles are due to the traumatic events in your past and the way that the human mind evolved to cope with issues like these.

You may already have begun to learn about PTSD if you're aware of the trauma that's impacted your ability to function. Complex PTSD is less known to most people, so you might or might not have run across it in your reading. It's usually the result of traumatic events such as sexual or physical abuse in childhood, domestic abuse, or living in chaotic environments or as a refugee. You're probably not sure where to start healing, or even if it's possible.

Although you might not have anyone close to you who is suffering due to a similar situation, there are others who are. You're not alone in your pain. Fortunately, researchers now know a lot about PTSD and Complex PTSD, and better yet, how to treat them. In this book you'll learn about your condition and what you can do to unwind these pathways in your brain.

You'll understand why you have the physical, emotional, and mental symptoms that have been plaguing you. There are exercises and suggestions to help you regain control over your life, so that you can start moving forward instead of being held back by frightening memories.

The first chapter is dedicated to what PTSD really is, and the difference between it and Complex PTSD. You'll learn a little about the history of the term and how the medical field treats these diseases. They lead to a number of other conditions if left untreated, and you'll learn what those are as well. As you discover more about the typical ways in which Complex PTSD manifests in your body and mind, you'll realize how much earlier events have affected your development.

Then you'll learn about how people get Complex PTSD and how it develops. It's true that two people can experience the same traumatic event and one may end up with a disorder and the other won't. It's not because the one who is ill is weak or mentally disturbed, but rather some brain wiring that isn't working properly.

Those who develop a traumatic disorder experience what's known as the "trauma loop" which begins with the experience and activates the "fight-or-flight" reactions in the brain. But with the disorder, the brain doesn't come out of the defensive reaction and continues to loop through the memories and defenses.

Next, you'll learn about the symptoms of PTSD. Though trauma disorders are primarily located in the brain, many if not most people also suffer physically. You may find that some of your illnesses or bodily aches are actually manifestations of your trauma, and not due to some other cause.

The difference between PTSD and Complex PTSD is mainly the inability to regulate or control your emotions. This is known as *affect dysregulation*, and you'll understand how it impacts your life. Typically, it appears in one of two forms. Either you're under-regulated, which often shows up as a lack of impulse control, or you're over-regulated and shut down feelings or reject them outright. If you don't clearly remember the trauma that happened when you were young, dysregulation is probably a factor.

In addition to emotional difficulties, you likely have a negative concept of yourself as a person as a result of your experiences. You have self-destructive thoughts that up until now you haven't been able to reframe, which leaves you with low self-esteem and feelings of guilt and shame. You'll find out where these concepts come from, and more importantly, how to deal with them in a constructive way so that you can begin thinking more positively.

You'll further discover why you've had so much difficulty in relationships. It's very common for those with Complex PTSD to lack fulfilling and intimate bonds with other people, whether romantic or platonic. Since most people need these connections for happiness and even survival, it's vital that you learn how to establish trust with others so that you can eventually develop these bonds. In chapter six you'll find some methods for opening up and moving forward.

Finally, you'll discover what recovery means and looks like for trauma survivors. There are more suggestions for tactics you can use to heal and avoid the trauma loop. You'll be able to improve your ability to assess the situation objectively and find the facts, which will help you take your anxiety out of the equation and let your logical brain take over. This allows your brain to exit its fight-or-flight mode.

At this point, you might be wondering if I'm an expert on the subject of healing from trauma, and why you should trust what I have to say. I am the survivor of a traumatic upbringing, with an abusive and manipulative parent. I spent years suffering from anxiety, mood swings, panic attacks, and all the other issues you've probably experienced as well.

Fortunately for me, I was able to recognize that my symptoms were the result of PTSD and I began to research the subject. Through my study, I was able to develop healing and coping strategies that helped me leave the trauma loop behind. What I learned made such a huge difference in my life that I wanted to share it with others who are going through their own traumatic journey.

I love helping others identify and recover from relationship and behavior patterns that are toxic and unbalanced, just as I have. In fact, everything you're about to discover about achieving a sense of freedom and self-worth is based on my own journey of overcoming PTSD and finding peace.

Because I'm so excited to be able to help you move forward, I want to encourage you to get started right away. The longer you put off reading the rest of the book, the longer you'll feel frustrated by daily occurrences that other people seem to be automatically able to deal with. You'll delay your understanding of how you got here and how you can escape your painful present. By starting right away instead, you'll overcome your difficulties that much sooner. You'll be able to form strong bonds and a support system that's there for you when you need it. So, let's get to it!

"You can't patch a wounded soul with a Band-Aid."

— MICHAEL CONNELLY

1

WHAT IS COMPLEX TRAUMA?

The word "trauma" is used a lot in popular culture. It sometimes refers to a type of hospital care, and sometimes it's used to describe an ordeal. However, Post-Traumatic Stress Disorder is a specific diagnosis with a specific meaning of the word "trauma." Complex PTSD is a very particular type of condition and comes with its own symptoms and results. Understanding what trauma really is and how Complex PTSD is separate from PTSD will help you view your condition from the proper perspective.

WHAT IS TRAUMA?

The standard dictionary definition is "an experience that produces psychological injury or pain."[1] However, by this benchmark, even relatively small incidents such as being ignored by someone you thought was your friend, or having a romantic partner decide to walk away, could be considered trauma!

For the purposes of this book and the diagnosis of PTSD, instead I'll use the more specific claim of a semi-permanent change in the person's nervous system due to a psychological or physical injury or event. In other words, the effect of the trauma incident is strong enough to actually alter the person's body, not just cause a brief pang of sadness or despair.

Many trauma events occur once and their duration is a short period of time, such as having a car accident, being mugged, or the death of a loved one. Other traumatic events that many people go through include:

- Divorce
- Losing a job
- Family/parental abandonment
- Abuse
- Assault
- Childbirth/surgery complications
- Incarceration
- Witnessing a crime, death, or other accident
- Other violence.

Almost everyone will experience one of these at least once in their lives, but not all who have suffered such an event will go on to develop any form of PTSD. Later in the book you'll learn more about the factors that may increase your likelihood of developing PTSD or

Complex PTSD. They include repeated or ongoing trauma, such as domestic abuse.

The human body and mind go through a certain natural process after a traumatic ordeal, and some of these reactions are similar to PTSD. In fact, the disorder has to be diagnosed after a period of thirty days following the event because the symptoms are so similar. For people who don't go on to develop PTSD, these natural reactions decrease over time until they're back to baseline as they were before the event.

Always on guard (hypervigilance)

Your mind is trying to protect you from experiencing another trauma, so it's especially aware of potential dangers and threats in your environment. This feels very strange for many people who have never been particularly concerned or aware of the perils around them, but it doesn't mean you're going crazy. It's just a natural consequence of going through an ordeal.

The hypervigilance doesn't have to be related to the actual event. For example, suppose you've recently gone through a divorce. You might be walking down a sidewalk at dusk, as you've done many times before, but you hear footsteps behind you and start to panic that someone's after you. Your brain is more sensitive to any kind of threat after a traumatic event, even things that never previously bothered you.

Unwanted thoughts or memories of the event

Typically, these are triggered by something that reminds you of the event. It can be anything: a person, a smell, a noise, a place, etc. These can occur as flashbacks or any other kind of memory. Again, this isn't a sign that you're going crazy or that anything is wrong with you. It's a response that happens because of the way our brains are wired (more about that in the next chapter!)

If you were in a car accident where you were hit by a white SUV, for example, you might have flashbacks every time you see a white SUV on the road. Or if you had a pine air freshener in your car, that scent could trigger a memory, whether you're in someone else's car or in a store that has pine-scented candles. If you had a passenger in your car, the subsequent sight of that person might trigger an intrusive memory.

It's not possible to know ahead of time what the trigger will be, but when the memories come up, recognize that they're related to the trauma itself.

Being on edge (hyperarousal)

You'll feel keyed up after an ordeal because your brain is preparing you to take action. Threats seem like they're everywhere, because when you're in this state of hyperarousal you're better able to react to danger. The hormones and physical reactions that accompany this state are perfectly fine when they occur from time to time or dissipate after a period of time. It's only when they're chronic that they can do long-lasting damage to your system.

Just as with hypervigilance, you're on edge about things that may or may not relate directly to the event that you endured. After a divorce, for example, you might be on edge every time you walk down the sidewalk that you previously never thought about. Or if you're in a grocery store and someone gets too close to you, your body might start the fight-or-flight reaction process.

Feeling endangered

Traumatic events leave you feeling unsafe. It may have been a physical event such as an assault or a car accident. Or it could be something like a death or divorce that leaves you feeling unsafe emotionally, because a part of your identity has just been taken away. Before the event, the world probably seemed like a reasonably safe and secure place, but now that illusion has been destroyed.

Many people feel that no place is safe after such an event, and so almost any location or situation seems dangerous. Even if you previously felt fine there, it now may fill you with anxiety or appear threatening to you. It's particularly common in places that remind you of the ordeal you went through.

For example, if you were assaulted in a park behind some trees, you may no longer feel safe in a forest or park where you don't have a clear view of your surroundings. Or you might not feel safe in a small grocery store where the space is tight, and you can't see over the shelves to scan for threats.

POST-TRAUMATIC STRESS DISORDER (PTSD)

While the symptoms in the last section are typical for anyone who's experienced trauma, there are additional factors that lead to a diagnosis of PTSD. These reactions are typically more extreme for those with PTSD, compared to the people who will find their symptoms decreasing over time and eventually returning to their "normal" state of being.

People who are likely to develop PTSD may find themselves with three additional behaviors on top of the reactions noted above.[2] Anyone who's experienced a trauma should be on the lookout for overdoing them to ensure that they reach out for help.

Avoidance

While it's pretty natural to avoid anything that reminds you of your ordeal, you can cross the line into avoiding anything and everything. That's what is likely to result in the disorder.

For example, someone who's experienced a mugging in a dark alley will avoid dark alleys for some time after the event. This is a normal reaction. Avoidance becomes a problem when the person starts avoiding any places where dark alleys exist, such as an entire town or city. Or won't go anywhere in the dark.

Once you get started on avoidance, you may find that you start avoiding more and more until you end up isolating yourself. It's one thing when a specific part of the world is dangerous and you avoid it, and something else when the entire world is dangerous, and you must avoid it.

Loss of interest

It's normal to feel a little reluctant to try new things in the aftermath of a traumatic event. The unknown is a little scary anyway, even before you've endured an ordeal. It's a problem when you don't want to do the things that you previously enjoyed.

If you're a dog owner who enjoys taking your dog on walks or to the dog park, no longer wanting to do that is a sign of depression. Or you might no longer want to hang out with your friends at a favorite cafe. Being detached from your interests in activities and people can also cause you to isolate. Then you'll lose the social support that you need after a trying time, which can lead to an eventual PTSD diagnosis.

Unhealthy coping strategies

These typically go along with avoidance. You don't want to have those intrusive memories anymore, or feel like you're in danger all the time. You may end up trying to numb yourself with substances, or other unhealthy behavior like shopping too much or gambling.

These behaviors might make you feel okay or numb for a short period of time, but of course after a while the effects wear off and you need to numb again. That's how these types of things can easily spiral into addiction.

They also don't help you solve your problem or heal yourself, so it's very easy to end up with PTSD when you can't curb your habits. Instead of diminishing over time, the reactions and thoughts that you're trying to avoid using substances or shopping actually grow stronger over time, not weaker.

Those who are diagnosed with PTSD may end up with some additional conditions as well. One study found that those with PTSD were eight times more likely to have three or more other diagnosed disorders during their lifetime, such as substance abuse, mood disorders like major depression or anxiety, and personality conditions like borderline personality disorder.[3] These are known as comorbid conditions.

There are specific criteria for diagnosing the existence of PTSD. The World Health Organization (WHO)/International Classification of Diseases (ICD) states that the disorder has developed when the person is having difficulties with functioning in daily life in terms of school, work, in the social sphere, or at home and has at least one of the following three responses.[4] Note that if the person is still able to function, or experiences only one or two of the following symptoms, the diagnosis of PTSD is not warranted.

1. Re-experiencing

Memories or thoughts of the trauma continue to occur. This can be through repeated nightmares related to the event, flashbacks, or unwanted memories in conjunction with feelings of severe fear or horror. While the occasional flashback or nightmare is common, those with PTSD can't seem to get rid of them.

2. Avoidance

Deliberately avoiding any kind of thought, memory, feeling, situation, or activity related to the event is also a symptom of PTSD. While common in the month following an ordeal for anyone, someone with the disorder does their best to pretend that nothing happened and to avoid anything that might remind them of the event for a longer period of time.

Keeping yourself too busy or preoccupied to think about what happened is another way of avoiding the trauma. It also can lead to blocking out parts of the event, or even the entire thing.

3. Hyperarousal

Being jumpy, easily startled, or excessively vigilant when it comes to threats for longer than a month after the event is also a part of the PTSD diagnosis.

This can interfere with sleep and concentration because any little thing can wake a PTSD sufferer up or distract them from their task. They may also be more irritable than usual as a consequence of constantly being jittery or on edge.

In the United States, the fundamental handbook for psychiatric disorders is the Diagnostic and Statistical Manual of Mental Disorders, known as the DSM. It's periodically updated and currently we're on version V, so you might have seen the DSM-V referenced in your research. The DSM-V largely agrees with WHO/ICD on the symptoms that lead to a diagnosis of PTSD, but they do differ slightly when it comes to Complex PTSD.

COMPLEX PTSD AND DIAGNOSIS

The idea of Complex PTSD, or C-PTSD, is more recent than PTSD itself. In 1988 Dr. Judith Herman of Harvard University suggested that a different diagnosis was necessary for repeated or ongoing trauma, which can cause more severe psychological harm than the single occurrence types of events that typically lead to PTSD. Trauma that occurs over a longer period of time or repeats itself is known as *complex*, and experiencing complex trauma is more likely to result in C-PTSD.

You'll learn more about these situations and their harm in a later chapter. However, the following are some examples of ordeals that may cause even more psychological damage.

- Domestic violence or abuse
- Human trafficking
- Neglect during childhood
- Extremely chaotic and/or violent environments, such as a living in a nation at war
- Being a refugee.

Originally, the exploration of C-PTSD was mainly on childhood trauma, particularly sexual abuse. Yet as research continued, it became clear that the duration of the ordeal, or how long it was endured, is a better predictor of C-PTSD compared to the nature of the trauma (e.g., childhood abuse.) When the trauma continues for a longer period of time, the survivor is under chronically high levels of stress and remains anxious and captive, either emotionally or physically. This set of factors results in the more severe harm experienced by those with complex trauma.

In the DSM-V, C-PTSD is not considered its own separate diagnosis, but is grouped under Disorders of Extreme Stress, Not Otherwise Specified (DESNOS). There are a variety of symptoms that fall under the DESNOS criteria after a traumatic event.

Difficulty regulating emotions or impulses

Being able to adapt emotions to the situation you're in is key for emotional regulation and an important factor in being emotionally intelligent. People who are traumatized are often unable to adjust to their current circumstances and express their emotions in a positive way.

Having issues with impulse control can show up in a number of ways. You might find yourself having unusual amounts of angry outbursts, taking too many risks, or being sexually promiscuous. Or you might end up directing these impulses inward and engaging in self-destructive behavior or becoming preoccupied with suicidal thoughts.

Before the event, you may have had a high EQ (emotional intelligence) and been able to regulate your emotions appropriately. The aftermath of your experience has badly affected your EQ. Or you may have had difficulties prior to your trauma as well, which have become worse as a consequence.

Changes in consciousness and focus

The typical response here is amnesia or having entire blocks of time wiped from your memory (even if only temporarily). It tends to come on suddenly, and it can last a few brief minutes or for months.

Or you may feel disconnected from your own body, your emotions, or the world around you. This symptom is also associated with feeling like you've lost your identity or sense of self, or you're confused about who you are. It's known as transient dissociative episodes or depersonalization.

In order to be diagnosed with DESNOS you'll experience at least one of these alterations.

Self-perception issues

Most people have some issues with how they perceive themselves from time to time, and this is not a disorder but a feature of life. For example, someone who's just been broken up with might feel unworthy or ineffective. For someone without a disorder, these feelings go away in a relatively short period of time.

In contrast, those with a DESNOS diagnosis have poor perceptions of themselves most of the time, which prevents them from living a so-called "normal" life. They feel ineffective or that they're permanently psychologically damaged. There is usually guilt and shame, especially around the traumatic event.

They don't think anyone else is going through what they've gone through and won't understand. This type of thinking, while common in C-PTSD, makes them more isolated and less likely to reach out for the help that they need. At least two of these issues with self-perception, as described above, must be present for the diagnosis.

Difficulty relating to other people

There are a variety of ways in which this difficulty manifests in C-PTSD sufferers, and at least one must be active to be diagnosed. One of the symptoms is the inability to trust other people.

Human beings are naturally social animals, even the introverts. You'll learn a bit more about that later in the book. Since we are social animals, we depend on the bonds we have with other humans to be healthy. Those connections can only be established with mutual trust and respect. Therefore, someone who has lost the ability to trust as a result of their disorder is cut adrift from what can help keep them healthy.

Another response is known as *re-victimization*. This is what happens when the C-PTSD sufferer continues to be a victim, or repeatedly endures victimization after the first trauma. Although popular culture often places the blame squarely on the victim, the extreme distress caused by the original trauma results in defense mechanisms that don't work as intended and leave them open to further harm.

Research shows that the best predictor of future trauma is a history of previous trauma. Children who are abused often grow up to be revictimized as a teen and/or later in adulthood (Fadelici, 2020.)[5]

Guilt over the ordeal often makes people pay attention only to their own thoughts and feelings, which causes them to ignore red flags or threats from others in their environment. Shame often results in isolation, which increases the likelihood of being vulnerable in a way that ends in re-victimization.

The other side of the coin is that the sufferer victimizes others, instead of being re-victimized. This helps them retain a sense of control over their own lives.

Physical symptoms

Although many people often think of mind and body as being two separate entities, in reality these two are very tightly connected. The brain sends signals to the body, but the body also provides feedback to the brain. Those who have C-PTSD often experience *somatization*, or the appearance of physical reactions to their trauma.

Did you know that you have neurons (nerve cells) in your gut? That's part of the reason the disorder may show up in the digestive system with pain or another condition. Additional reactions include chronic pain, cardiovascular symptoms like high blood pressure and inflammation, and sexual ones such as loss of sex drive.

The diagnosis of DESNOS requires the patient to have at least two of the physical symptoms, or somatization.

Changes in understanding the meaning of life

At least one of these reactions is necessary as DESNOS criteria. Some people have an overwhelming feeling of despair or hopelessness. They cannot even imagine a world in which hope exists, or that they themselves are able to heal. It seems like all their symptoms whether physical, mental, or emotional will never go away or dissipate in intensity and there's nothing to live for.

Another way that this reaction shows up is in a complete loss of faith or other sustaining beliefs. After a difficult event, many people may undergo a temporary loss of faith or anger towards a deity or spiritual ideal. But those with C-PTSD have a chronic loss of belief and can't see how they would ever make it back to their previous spiritual or foundational practice.

Unlike in the DSM-V, C-PTSD is recognized as its own disorder by the WHO/ICD. In addition to the three criteria for PTSD of re-experience, avoidance, and heightened threat awareness, C-PTSD sufferers also experience all three of the following:

1. Inability to manage or control the duration or intensity of "negative" emotions such as anger, fear, and sadness (known as affect dysregulation)
2. Negative concept of themselves
3. Inability to trust others.

You can see that these overlap with the DESNOS diagnosis. Ultimately, identifying many psychological or mental conditions is not an exact science, whether you're using WHO/ICD or DSM-V criteria. However, it's clear what kinds of issues accompany the aftermath of trauma and result in PTSD or C-PTSD. If these symptoms and reactions are preventing you from functioning in your daily life, you'll need to learn to heal from and cope with your ordeal. Fortunately, research has shown us the way to recovery.

CHAPTER SUMMARY

The human body and brain produce certain reactions to traumatic events that are common for everyone who experiences a car crash, death of a loved one, etc. Those with trauma who are unable to return to baseline may be diagnosed with PTSD, and those whose ordeals last for a long time or repeat are at risk for C-PTSD.

- Trauma causes changes to a person's nervous system, and

may be the result of a divorce, abuse, and other events including witnessing a crime or accident.

- Common symptoms of trauma include being very aware of threats, hypersensitivity to the environment, intrusive memories and thoughts of the event, and feeling unsafe.
- The common symptoms may dissipate over a month or so, as they do for many survivors, or they may intensify and interfere with daily life, in which case a Post-Traumatic Stress Disorder diagnosis is often warranted.
- PTSD is accompanied by other symptoms as well, and generally is a consequence of a trauma that occurs once and for a finite period of time, such as a car accident or assault.
- Longer-term or repeated traumas may develop instead into C-PTSD, which can be more severe and has additional symptoms.

In the next chapter you will learn how and where C-PTSD comes from.

2

WHERE DOES C-PTSD COME FROM?

I t's important for anyone experiencing C-PTSD to understand what's going on in their brain and body, which is helpful in the process of healing from the trauma. These symptoms are a consequence of how the human brain evolved and how it works in some people. Even up until the last century, scientists believed that the brain couldn't generate new nerve cells (neurons). Fortunately, we've since discovered that's not true. Which is great news because it means that you can potentially make changes to your brain to make recovery possible!

If you think of yourself as a car—especially a newer model that has an electric or partially electric engine and technologies such as parallel parking assist or drift warnings—your brain is the engine, and the rest of the car is your body. Let's pop open the hood and take a good look at the engine and how it works.

HOW THE HUMAN BRAIN EVOLVED

You might remember (or not) from your school science class that humans, Homo Sapiens, evolved on the African savannah. At the time, humans had to defend against predators that might kill us, and also had to find ways to feed ourselves. Those who did so the best were the ones that survived to pass their genes onto the next generation, so those of us here now are the descendants of the humans that best adapted to their environment.

Due to the way that we evolved and survived as a species, our minds and bodies were shaped by the environment. Just a reminder, again from science class, that evolution happens over many generations, not just one or two. A generation for Homo Sapiens is about twenty years. Therefore, a century is only about five generations. The surroundings in which most people now live began with the Industrial Revolution, which was in the 1700s. So, we've really only lived this way for three hundred years, roughly fifteen generations, and the recent technology explosion is only a generation or two ago.

The consequence of this is that the human brain evolved to fight off predators on the African savannah, and we're using them in an environment where we have no predators (except maybe each other!) and we have a very different life from our ancestors. We're constantly on the go, checking our technology, working long hours because we're not tethered to daylight anymore, and consuming whatever we want. We don't have to hunt down our food, and calories are plentiful.

But that's not what the human brain adapted for. We survived in small groups of about 150 people or so, because bringing down large predators is a pack activity. Not something one person can do on their own. Back then we didn't have supermarkets and didn't know where the next meal would come from. The human brain thus evolved to finding sweet, fatty, and salty tastes very pleasing, because that meant we'd be able to get enough calories.

Also, as a result of not knowing where the next meal is coming from, the human brain likes to conserve energy as much as possible. That way you're not out there burning too many calories and starving to death when you might not eat again for many days. Obviously, this has led to some physical health issues for modern people, particularly in the developed world where calories are plentiful, but there are also repercussions for the modern brain as well.

Because the human brain is basically still back in the savannah, it treats all threats as the same. It can't tell the difference between a life-threatening situation and one that is scary but probably won't kill you. If you are afraid that you're going to be fired, for example, your brain thinks you're about to get eaten by a tiger and makes adjustments accordingly. Unfortunately, the survival instincts that worked very well on the savannah don't work so well in the modern world.

There are a number of ways that the brain can get things wrong, including systematic errors in thinking known as *cognitive bias*. These errors are baked into the brain as a result of how we evolved. In other words, it doesn't matter how intelligent you are, your brain automatically makes these mistakes.

For example, one bias is known as recency bias, where you weigh what happened recently more heavily than something that occurred further back in time. Suppose you've had depression before and were able to function with it through medication, or therapy, or both. Once it was successful, you might have dropped the therapy and been fine for a while. But recently you became depressed again, as commonly happens. But you'll think about your current depression more and not the previous time when you recovered from it, because the depression is what happened lately.

Another bias is to remember the negative more than the positive. You can see how that would have benefited ancient people, so they remembered what happened after they ate the wrong berry and wouldn't eat it again. Or avoid the place with all the hissing snakes in it. You can also see how that would make life more difficult for people who have a tendency toward depression or anxiety in the first place.

HOW THE BRAIN WORKS

All animal brains in the most basic sense work in the same way, through sending electrical or chemical signals that "tell" various organs or systems what to do. There are a lot of different sections in the brain responsible for a variety of things, most of which you're not aware of because they happen at the unconscious or subconscious level. (I'll be using these terms pretty much interchangeably.)

When it comes to survival, one of the key structures is the *amygdala*. It's a little almond-shaped part of the brain responsible for motivation and emotions, specifically fear. The amygdala is a part of the *limbic system* in your brain that deals with emotions and memories. (Some people refer to the limbic system as part of the "mammalian brain" which is more advanced than the lizard but not a thinking organ.)

If you're scared or feel threatened, the amygdala is on it. Sensory data can bypass your thinking structures and arrive directly at the amygdala for a faster response. This little area of the brain is responsible for the fight-or-flight reflex (sometimes also known as the fight-freeze-flight reflex.) When you're threatened and fearful, the amygdala helps prepare your body to escape (or kill) a predator. Remember, the brain is still back in the savannah and thinks fear means death is imminent.

There are a number of things that the brain does to get the body ready. The *sympathetic nervous system* in your brain and body is activated, causing hormones like cortisol and adrenaline to be released. This results in a faster heart rate, blood pressure, and breathing rate. Because you might have to sprint away from the predator that's threatening you. Blood is sent to your muscles, legs, and arms. Your focus tightens so you're paying more attention to the threat than to other things that may be going on around you.

Once this stress response has been activated, it normally takes 20 minutes to an hour to return to baseline, if it's functioning normally (Cherry, 2019).[1] Note that none of this is consciously controlled by you as it all happens automatically. Researchers now know that while the occasional stress response is perfectly fine for you (and can even help you do well in high-stress situations like a presentation or a race), chronically elevated stress hormones are dangerous to your health.

We share this structure with animal ancestors, as well as other parts of the brain that operate unconsciously, such as the regulation of body temperature, breathing rate, repair of cells while you sleep, and so forth. You might have heard of the "reptilian" or "lizard" brain, which is what all of these things are contained in. In his book *Thinking Fast and Slow*, the psychologist and economist Daniel Kahneman refers to the lizard brain as System 1.

Most of System 1 occurs subconsciously. Tasks are carried out without your conscious knowledge, including the generation of emotions, formation of memories, and reflex reactions. System 1 is fast. It works on rules of thumb (heuristics) so the brain can make quick decisions.

Very important when you're on the savannah and you see some grass waving. Your brain will guess that it's a tiger ready to eat you and prepare you accordingly. If it turns out that it was just the wind, that's fine. You survived either way, and in ancient times the stress response didn't have much of a downside. After you escaped, everything would settle down.

What your brain doesn't want is for you to stand around trying to figure out what you should do. The likelihood is that you'd die (when faced with a hungry predator) and your brain would really prefer you to survive, thank you very much. It doesn't want you to try to make long lists of pros and cons of what would happen if the grass is or is not hiding a tiger, or consider the advantages and disadvantages of fleeing.

Those kinds of reasoning decisions are made with System 2, which includes the human part of the brain that people use for logic, thinking, and reasoning. It is much slower than System 1—agonizingly slow when you're faced with a tiger about to eat you—and it is an energy hog in comparison.

Much of our logical thought processes are contained in the prefrontal cortex, which is connected to the limbic system and is integral to higher-level, *Homo Sapiens* thinking. It's where self-awareness is located, the regulation of emotion occurs, and where conscious beliefs sit, among other things. The prefrontal cortex doesn't mature until age 25, unlike other human organs and systems which reach maturity significantly earlier. This is the part of the brain that typical modern humans need the most in order to function in the 21st century.

It was long thought that people arrived at logical, "modern" decisions through careful analysis, rational thinking, and so forth. Hence lists of pros and cons when trying to decide whether to take a new job in a different location, the comparison of advantages and disadvantages of new vs. old, and other reasoning tools that people use. In this model, the prefrontal cortex and higher-level thinking of the conscious mind were the drivers on decisions like these.

However, we recently discovered that this is mostly not true. It turns out that decisions are mostly made at the subconscious level, based on emotions (Camp, 2012).[2] A neuroscientist discovered that people with damage to their emotional centers could not make decisions, even after considering pros and cons of one option versus another. Conscious decision-making is basically after-the-fact justification for whichever choice the subconscious made. (Advertisers know this and try to hook you with emotion, before providing the facts and features that will satisfy the logical part of the brain.) The fact that emotions come first is key to understanding why C-PTSD can develop in some people.

As you might imagine, all that logical thinking, which is a fairly recent evolutionary project, takes up a lot of resources in terms of energy (calories). Recall that earlier you learned that the human brain evolved to conserve energy. Therefore, it tends to default to System 1, which is faster and uses up fewer resources. In other words, your brain prefers to use heuristics for rapid decisions rather than logical thinking. Most importantly in any discussion about anxiety or emotional regulation, when you're under threat, whether physical or psychological, the brain tends to shut System 2 off. Rational thinking is unnecessary for survival on the savannah when faced with a hungry tiger. Energy is shifted to the stress response so you can get away from the predator quickly.

Most of us in the developed world face more psychological threats than physical ones, yet our brain still treats threats as though they're physical. When System 2 is offline, you can't really think through the consequences of your actions. You can't regulate your emotions or control their expression very well. Even though the modern world requires more use of the human brain and logical reasoning, when you feel under threat, you're at the mercy of emotions and autonomic reflexes.

In addition to emotions, the amygdala plays a part in processing memories. Another part of the brain's limbic system which is also involved in memories is the hippocampus, which is mainly responsible for short-term or episodic memories. Though they both can act independently, these two brain areas can also team up. Memories are better recalled when they're stored along with an emotion (either good or bad), so the amygdala and hippocampus help form long-term memories.

THE BRAIN AND TRAUMA

After a traumatic experience, the sympathetic nervous system (SNS), including the amygdala, remains on high alert. This is why everyone experiences things like hypervigilance and hyperarousal after an ordeal. With normal functioning, the SNS will gradually return to baseline and stress levels dissipate. If they don't, and the SNS remains stuck in the trauma response, the entire brain is in stress mode, which affects the physical body as well.

Being constantly in a high state of arousal from trauma response, the amygdala is constantly reacting to potential threats and danger that it continues to search out. When your body is constantly at a high threat level, it has a hard time regulating itself. Your body gets tired, because producing all the stress response takes a lot of energy. Stress hormones make the brain's hippocampus less effective at consolidating memories, which means the brain has difficulty receiving the signal that the danger is over. In addition, these effects on the hippocampus may cause the brain to suppress the memory of the ordeal in order to cope with it. All of these issues occur at the subconscious level, so they're not anything that you have control over.

There are a variety of unconscious operations that happen during sleep, from encoding learning from the day to making repairs on the cellular level. They're all necessary for mental and physical health. Although many people in the 21st century may brag about how little sleep they get, they're doing themselves quite a disservice. Often those with PTSD and C-PTSD have difficulty sleeping as a result of the disorder.

One of the things that happens in the brain during sleep is the maintenance of neural pathways in the brain. This is a part of habit formation as well. Pathways that go unused will be pruned back (so they don't waste unnecessary energy) and pathways that are used are strengthened and may eventually become habits. Because clearly something that's being often used must be important!

Unfortunately, of course, for those suffering from all forms of PTSD, the pathways that are being strengthened during the sleep you do get are the negative ones that result in poor self-perception, increased startle response, and so forth. The brain responds to the trauma that has occurred in ways that will protect it (and you), but when it can't return to a normal state the protection won't work the way it's designed to.

Another consequence of complex trauma is that it can alter people all the way down to the genetic level. We all have genetic inheritances from our parents through DNA, which sometimes includes genes that have been implicated in diseases like Alzheimer's and dementia, certain cancers, and others.

However, not everyone who has a copy of these genes will actually contract the disease. In the last century you might have heard of the debate between nature vs. nurture, or whether DNA (nature) has more influence on a person's life than their upbringing (nurture). It's a bit more complicated than that, as it turns out. The environment that a person lives in and other outside influences can turn some genes on or off. Some people with a DNA inheritance of dementia don't get the disease because those genes aren't turned on.

One of the factors that can alter gene expression is complex trauma. Those with C-PTSD, as you learned in the last chapter, are more likely to be diagnosed with additional illnesses. This might be a potential result of trauma switching genes on or off. Fortunately, the gene expression of on or off is based on chemical signaling. While you can't change your DNA, you may be able to change the signaling that was affected by trauma.

Complex trauma is not just the ordeal that someone has gone through. It's also their fixation on it, and the compulsive return to the terror and drama over and over again. When you have C-PTSD, the brain can't let go of stress responses or return to normal, so instead the emotions repeat and become reinforced.

WHEN THE BRAIN CAN'T LET GO

At the end of a life-threatening situation, a healthy nervous system will "finish" the fight-or-flight response by literally shaking off the additional energy generated. The limbic system sends a signal that causes shaking or trembling (which is where "shaking like a leaf" after a fright comes from). This tells the body that the threat is gone and that the stress response is no longer necessary. Then the nervous system returns to normal.

You can see this in animals—after they're triggered by a threat, they will shake themselves to rid their bodies of the excess energy. If animals are unable to shake off their ordeal and return their nervous systems back to normal, they might actually die (Shaw, 2019).[3] By contrast, humans tend to become ill.

In people with C-PTSD, their brains form what's known as a trauma loop. You've already learned that after a trauma, the brain fires up its defenses, especially the fight-or-flight reflex. It's the resulting patterns afterward that determine whether the trauma leads to C-PTSD. In short, the loop looks like this:

- Stress response activated
- If situation dealt with, return to normal (no PTSD)
- If not, stress response still active and emotions build
- If emotions build long enough, sense of helplessness/being overwhelmed triggers inertia defenses: submit or become hopeless
- If the brain submits, defenses deactivated, and brain returns to normal (no PTSD)
- If it becomes hopeless, defenses remain activated
- If defenses remain activated and brain cannot find a way to be safe, they are permanently activated and continue to loop, leading to C-PTSD.

You can see, going step by step, how the brain's survival mechanisms can turn against us in certain situations. After the trauma occurs and the fight-or-flight reflex is activated, you can become more afraid, rather than shaking off the danger after it's gone. This often occurs for trauma that goes on for a long time or repeatedly, since the brain must stay in stress response for longer periods of time. It can also happen when the person feels that they can't escape or fight the situation. There's no way to "finish" the SNS arousal because neither fight nor flight is possible.

Consider someone who is the victim of domestic abuse. Most abusers can be charming, which is how they are able to attract their victims, and they don't abuse their partners all the time. The victim's stress response is nearly always present, because they tend to walk on eggshells around the violent partner in the hopes of avoiding being a target. Even when the partner isn't currently lashing out.

Or someone who's living in a war-torn country. There's no safety available anywhere within the borders, and so staying alive means that the person must constantly be on high alert for threats. The brain isn't able to dismiss the stress response, because the danger simply does not go away unless the person is able to find refuge somewhere else. Though being a refugee is also a factor for developing PTSD, because they're traveling to places they're unfamiliar with, and the brain can't relax its vigilance when constantly dealing with the unknown.

These are just a few examples of how people can be in situations where their brains are on high alert for danger over long periods of time. It's not something that our early ancestors really had to deal with, because they'd run away from or fight the predator and deal with the situation. Afterwards their nervous systems, no longer faced with imminent threat, could signal that the episode was over, and they were safe.

For our ancestors, feeling the fear and responding appropriately took care of the matter. But for modern humans, it doesn't always work that way. C-PTSD develops over time, because it takes time for a stressed brain to believe that there is no way out and no hope of escape. That's why the duration of the ordeal is more important than how it occurred.

Feeling like you're under constant threat and having your body constantly pumping out stress hormones to prepare for fight or flight doesn't just cause physical harm, but emotional harm as well. With your body's lizard brain activated, it's harder to think rationally about anything, including the specific situation in which you find yourself. Recall that emotions come first, and so in these circumstances, fear can lead to anger, frustration, discontent, and sometimes more fear.

As these emotions wash over you frequently, you may feel overwhelmed and overcome by a sense of helplessness. These feelings trigger more intense emotional defenses. Your brain wants you to survive so it can survive, and it will try to find solutions to avoid being in danger. But at this point, escaping the situation isn't possible and you're no longer capable of initiating action. Instead, the brain ends up thinking that submitting to what's going on is best, or maybe becoming immobilized will save you.

Now your brain has left behind the defenses of arousal (fighting or fleeing) and is activating defenses designed for inertia, like collapsing or fainting. You've still got plenty of emotions roiling around, like anger, disdain, and hatred yet still need safety, which means sadness, pain, and defeat. Typically, at this inflection point there are two options: one is to submit, and the other is to become hopeless.

1. Submit

If you accept the situation as it is and are able to control the fear and sense of hopelessness, the brain recognizes this as a threat reduction and will stop raising its defenses. In time, your system will return to baseline. Similarly, if you see a way out through the submission, your brain will deactivate the defenses.

For example, someone who is being abused will stop resisting and attempt to do everything they're told. They may make plans to leave or even take revenge against their abuser, which also deactivates the inertia defenses. Over time their stress response will return to normal, though this may take months to years.

2. Become hopeless

When the terror and exhaustion are too overwhelming, a person can lose all hope instead. Unfortunately, this sense of hopelessness instructs the brain to continue to keep the stress response going. So, you'll keep those defenses activated and lose sight of everything except survival, no matter the cost.

When someone can't find a way to stay or feel safe, when they can't think of a way out of their circumstances, the defenses will stay permanently activated. They're in self-defeating survival mode, rather than able to find a way out. This is what causes the typical symptoms of the disorder of numbing, disassociating, depersonalization, memory loss, and others. The brain is doing what it takes to keep going, and these symptoms are all methods of survival for someone who's lost all hope with eternally raised mental defenses.

You may have heard of the saying, "neurons that fire together wire together." The more often the trauma loop is repeated, the stronger the neural pathways of the loop become. The brain strengthens the pathways because they're being used more often, which embeds the loop even more deeply into the mind.

The brain learns to function under these conditions and the repetition of this loop between emotions and defenses is what creates complex trauma. The constant release of stress hormones destabilizes other bodily functions such as digestion, sweating, heart rate, and others.

With complex trauma, you're eternally on high alert with no one to trust and no hope for your future. This loop of traumatization affects not just your physical health, but your perception of yourself and the world around you, your emotions and your ability to reflect on your own thoughts and actions and other behaviors.

EFFECTS OF CONSTANT STRESS RESPONSE

As you read earlier, there are a number of things that occur in your mind and body when you experience hyperarousal for long periods of time. It strains your ability to adapt to your environment, which leads to a variety of health conditions. PTSD particularly affects the system that is known to lead to irritable bowel syndrome, fibromyalgia, and chronic fatigue when not functioning properly. It may be the cause of otherwise unexplained pain, especially in muscles and bones.

People with PTSD have higher rates of cardiovascular disease, especially with high blood pressure (McFarlane, 2010).[4] They also tend to have high cholesterol and triglycerides, which often develops into cardiovascular and other diseases. PTSD is a risk factor in obesity, which is another precursor for illness. Individuals with high stress levels have an increased mortality rate compared to those who don't experience chronic stress response.

In addition to heart disease, PTSD sufferers also experience higher rates of other conditions, as the elevated stress response increases the risk for a number of other ailments. The hormone cortisol in particular has some well-known negative effects if the body continues to pump it out on a regular basis. Too much stress also contributes to additional inflammation throughout the body, which is a known factor for a number of unhealthy conditions (Hannibal, et al, 2014).[5]

Inflammation widens gaps in the barriers between blood and the brain, as well as those in the intestinal walls. These allow larger bodies and toxins to cross these barriers, causing further inflammation and damage. The dysfunctional cortisol responses are also linked to acquired immunodeficiency syndrome or AIDS (Ibid).[6]

Inflammation releases "free radicals," which are molecules containing oxygen and an odd number of electrons. The free radicals can then attach to and interfere with other molecules. Moderate amounts of free radicals actually help the body take care of itself, for example by allowing attaching to and destroying an invasive microbe (Pham-Huy et al, 2008).[7]

However, too many free radicals cause *oxidative stress*, which damages cell membranes and other structures within the cell. This leads to certain degenerative illnesses. Oxidative stress has been linked to certain kinds of cancers because it can alter the DNA of a cell and disrupt its behavior. In addition to smoking tobacco, the oxidative stress from inflammation caused by asbestos is known to contribute to lung cancer (Ibid).[8]

Too many free radicals and the resulting inflammation is also known to be a factor in lung (*pulmonary*) diseases such as asthma and chronic obstructive pulmonary disease (COPD). They are also known to affect the brain in a number of ways in addition to depression that lead to illness. Alzheimer's disease (and other forms of dementia), Parkinson's disease, multiple sclerosis and ALS or Lou Gehrig's disease.

Free radicals may also induce your cells to essentially turn on each other, which is what happens with auto-immune disorders. Your body no longer recognizes its own cells and believes them to be invaders, which it then tries to fight off as it would an actual invader. Rheumatoid arthritis is an autoimmune disease where joints and their tissues are continually inflamed, as an example.

Oxidative stress run rampant is also known to contribute to a variety of kidney (*renal*) diseases, such as chronic kidney failure. It can even damage your eyesight by inducing the formation of cataracts. It's a factor in additional systems throughout your body, including other cancers, diabetes, and premature cell aging. Your immune system also gets stressed out, which means you might be at higher risk for infections because your body can't fight off bacterial or viral invaders.

All the oxidative stress that your body endures with too many free radicals doesn't necessarily mean that you'll end up with any of these specific ailments. However, it makes you more likely to develop them over time compared to someone whose cortisol levels are functioning properly. Any and all of the conditions that are generated from an elevated stress response may also lead to bodily pain. It's important to understand that physical effects are a very real manifestation of the changes that occur when the brain is under constant stress and awash in hormones that are intended for short periods of time.

In addition to all the physical effects of PTSD, there are a number of mental ones as well. In a later chapter you'll learn more about the symptoms of PTSD and C-PTSD. The symptoms can also be effects that come on after a period of time in which the disorder hasn't been addressed or treated.

As with the physical effects, suffering from any form of PTSD doesn't mean that you will go through all of these situations. You're more likely to develop them if you have PTSD than not. Also, you may only have one of the following effects, or you may have more than one. There are a variety of factors that contribute to the disorder, and your particular combination isn't necessarily the same as anyone else's. How PTSD manifests and its results are different for each person.

Depression

Everyone feels "down" or "blue" some of the time, even if they're otherwise mentally healthy. Major or clinical depression is different from the garden-variety blues. Those with major depression can't function normally as a result of a continuous feeling of sadness and a loss of interest in activities or people that formerly brought happiness and pleasure.

Other symptoms of depression include weight changes that you didn't intend, because you may have a total loss of appetite or you might be hungry all the time. Your sleep is disturbed, meaning you might not be able to sleep well or in contrast that you sleep too much. It's sometimes accompanied by feelings of guilt and shame, and difficulty concentrating or thinking.

The occasional sleepless night or binge on ice cream when your date didn't go well is normal. It's when your symptoms continue for at least a couple of weeks that you could be diagnosed with depression.

Anxiety

Just as everyone gets the blues from time to time, everyone experiences anxiety at least sometimes. People who are otherwise mentally healthy get anxious before public speaking or before a date, or for some other event.

Anxiety disorders occur when the worry is persistent, especially about daily issues, and excessive or intense. The anxiety interferes with normal everyday functioning and are out of proportion to the actual (potential) danger of the situation.

Substance addiction

As noted earlier, substance problems and addictions are common coping mechanisms for many people, even those without PTSD. The preferred substance might produce euphoria or just a numbness, but either way it's a temporary fix.

The more you use and abuse the substance, the more those neural pathways get strengthened. That's why it's often easier for people who have been using it for a short time to quit the substance, because they haven't strengthened the pathway as much.

In addition, these substances alert the brain to pleasure, which means it releases happy neurochemicals like dopamine. The reward system of the brain, of which dopamine is a part, is a way to encourage pleasurable habits. When dopamine is released, the brain is essentially saying, Yes, we like this. Please do more of this!

You can see how that can lead to addiction, because your brain is telling you that it wants more of the substance. With many of them, you need more and more to get that dopamine release, so you need more and more substance to feel better.

Eating disorders

As with anxiety and depression, nearly everyone has "fat days" and feels like skipping food to get back on track. Or they overeat due to emotions, which may be pleasurable or not. It's the extreme behavior of attaining a specific body shape or weight control that marks eating disorders.

It sometimes represents a feeling of control for someone who otherwise feels that they don't have much control over their lives. But they can control how much they eat, or how much food is absorbed. Eating disorders develop over time and can start off as simply wanting to be a bit thinner (Jade, 2019).[9]

You might have heard of some of the disorders, such as anorexia nervosa, where the person severely controls their food intake. The guidelines for adult women are to consume 2,000 calories per day, more or less, depending on factors like height and how sedentary they are. Someone with anorexia usually tries to take in less than half that amount. You may also have heard of orthorexia, where someone begins eating healthy but then develops an obsession with healthy eating that interferes with their daily life.

On the other end of the spectrum are disorders such as binge eating disorder and bulimia. You may binge or overeat excessively and feel like you can't stop even when you've had enough. Bulimics tend to binge and purge, so that they can eat what they want but don't absorb the calories.

Self-harming

This can take a variety of expressions, but it too is a coping method for emotional pain, if not a healthy one. It's hurting yourself on purpose, which can (like some eating disorders) give you a sense of control in an otherwise chaotic life.

Those who self-harm may cut themselves with sharp objects, burn themselves, pick at hair or skin, and pick at wounds to prevent them from healing. It's not so much a mental illness as it is an unhealthy coping strategy. For some people, self-harm can stimulate their endorphins, so they (temporarily) feel better as a result.

Suicidal tendencies

Although most people don't talk about it, apparently plenty of human beings have fleeting thoughts of ending their lives sometimes. For those who are emotionally healthy, it doesn't leave a lasting impact and the person can easily move on.

But for others, especially those with PTSD, these tendencies can recur or be present for longer periods of time. This is obviously dangerous, because the combination of the tendency plus a means of ending life can have disastrous consequences.

People who do end up committing suicide usually can't think through the consequences of the action to consider how friends and family would be deeply upset. Or they may believe that they're all alone in the world and no one would miss them if they went, which is usually not the case.

Lack of social interaction

A support system is key for optimum health for human beings. Even introverts need a few people that they can count on, and extroverts tend to have more people in their social circles. Going it alone is mentally and emotionally difficult, and even people without PTSD have cognitive distortions that make them unable to see reality when they're alone for too long.

Because PTSD sufferers tend to feel guilt and shame (among other emotions), they also tend to withdraw from their friends and family.

Many also have depression, which means that the things they used to enjoy are no longer pleasurable. So, they stop going out and visiting friends or reaching out by telephone to their connections.

As with many other factors in PTSD, the longer you go without social support, the more difficult it is to restart it or get back in the swing of things.

For example, you might think of someone that you know casually. You might feel a little awkward about picking up the phone to call them. If you haven't called in a few weeks, picking up the phone is even harder than if you'd called them a few days ago. And if it's been months since you connected, you might feel so awkward that the phone is impossible to pick up.

With PTSD, this happens even with people you know well, or even love. You don't call them or pick up when they call. Maybe one day you're feeling like you might want to talk to them, but now it's been weeks or months. You're wondering how you're going to explain this gap in connection, and it seems so difficult that you decide to do it another day. Which never comes, because the distance grows the longer you wait.

Separation or divorce

Unfortunately, many people who don't have PTSD don't understand it or how it shows up in different people. If you have a partner who knows nothing about it except for what they see on TV, they might have a skewed perception.

Other partners might understand the disorder to a point, but not be able to cope with the symptoms that show up. Or think that what's going on is "all in your head," not recognizing that there are physical effects from PTSD as well.

Sometimes, people with PTSD act out in a way that their partners think is dangerous to them or their children, and they want to leave the marriage to ensure their family's safety.

Although separation and divorce don't typically help the PTSD sufferer heal, they are fairly common in these situations.

Lack of relationships

The inability to trust people that's associated with the disorder often results in having fewer connections with others, whether platonic as just friends or romantic. As noted earlier, social interaction is important, and having strong bonds with at least a couple of people is key for mental and emotional health.

PTSD interferes with these bonds when it's not treated. You feel like you can't trust others, and you withdraw from them. Close friends may continue to try for a while, but if you don't respond they may eventually give up, leaving you without a support system.

Without friends and partners, it's easier to isolate even more and get stuck in your own head. Which isn't a great place for PTSD sufferers to be.

In addition to these effects, PTSD often shows up in conjunction with other mood or mental disorders, known as *comorbidity*. These include eating disorders, other depression or anxiety illnesses, and

Obsessive-Compulsive Disorder (OCD). It's not always possible to tease out which one came first, but some of them are known to make a diagnosis of C-PTSD more likely in someone who has them compared to someone who doesn't, as you'll find out in the next section.

CONTRIBUTING FACTORS TO COMPLEX PTSD

Earlier we discussed the nature vs. nurture debate, and that C-PTSD can alter genes to the point of turning some off or on. Similarly, there are factors that can lead someone to be more susceptible to the disorder compared to others. Some are genetic in nature, but others are environmental. Not everyone who may be more genetically susceptible will end up with it, because they've received nurturing that essentially keeps those genes "off". Conversely, people are diagnosed with it without any genetic factors contributing.

History of anxiety or depression

Both having a family history and having a record of these conditions yourself is often found in people with C-PTSD. Being anxious or depressed and adding complex trauma is not a recipe for solid mental health!

Regulation of chemicals and hormones

Depending on how your brain releases chemicals and hormones, especially when under stress, you may have a higher likelihood of the disorder.

Tendency toward neuroticism

People who are "neurotic" tend to be moodier than average. They often feel anxious, worried, jealous, angry, frustrated, and/or lonely. Though every living person sometimes has these feelings, they're usually short in duration and easily dismissed for people who aren't very neurotic.

By contrast, neurotic people worry a lot. The emotions may be intense or last for a longer time period, or both. It's much harder for someone who is high in neuroticism to shake off these feelings or let the anxiety go. It's often an inherited trait, though it doesn't have to result in C-PTSD.

Repeated trauma in childhood

You learned that trauma over a long period of time, or repeated traumatic events, are more likely to lead to C-PTSD. Children can end up with the disorder as well as adults, especially since they're still learning coping skills.

Complex trauma interferes with learning how to deal with life too. It's unlikely that a child whose brain has been disrupted in this way is capable of processing later traumas in any kind of healthy way.

Lack of support system

After someone has experienced a traumatic event, it's important for them to process what happened in a way that's healthy. Being connected to other people also gives them a sense of hope, and a safe environment to process in.

Those who tend to cope with their lives by themselves, or without seeking out support, are more likely to develop the disorder (Tull, 2019).[10]

Dysfunctional family

When the family isn't a safe place to be, it's much more difficult for someone who's experienced trauma to work through it in a healthy way. This can be the family of origin, or current family.

Either way, the inability to heal the trauma is more likely to result in C-PTSD. You're with your family every day (for the most part) and living in a toxic or dysfunctional environment can be re-victimizing.

Dangerous job

Most of the original PTSD studies were done on military veterans. You may have heard of "shell shock," which many World War veterans came home with. Today we call that PTSD instead, but either way it can be understood as a response to the trauma of combat. My own grandfather (who was in combat in WWII) was known to have suffered shell shock. Similarly, combat seems to increase the likelihood of C-PTSD.

Other occupations that are more likely to lead to the disorder are law enforcement and firefighting.

CHAPTER SUMMARY

C-PTSD is actually a result of the way the human brain is wired to survive. When the stress response system is activated after a trauma and not able to shut itself off, the chronic load has a variety of mental, emotional, and physical effects.

- Though we live in the age of computer technology, our brains were designed to keep us alive on the savannah and to flee or fight when the fear circuit is activated.
- The human brain reacts to trauma with a stress response, which is supposed to deactivate when the danger is past.
- The stress response doesn't deactivate for a variety of reasons, and if the brain starts cycling through the trauma loop, the person is likely to develop PTSD or C-PTSD after a long period of time.
- Being on high alert causes a constant wash of stress hormones like cortisol, which can lead to diseases like diabetes, Alzheimer's, cardiovascular disease, cancer, and others.
- There are both genetic and environmental risk factors for C-PTSD which lead to a higher likelihood of having the disorder after trauma.

In the next chapter you will learn about the symptoms for PTSD, and later in the book you'll discover the additional C-PTSD symptoms in greater detail.

3

SYMPTOMS OF PTSD

Before we get into the specifics of Complex Post-Traumatic Stress Disorder, you need to be familiar with the symptoms of PTSD. You learned in an earlier chapter that to be diagnosed with C-PTSD, the symptoms of PTSD also must be present. In other words, everyone with the complex form of PTSD has PTSD, though not everyone with PTSD has C-PTSD. In this chapter you'll better understand what the signs of PTSD are and what they mean in real life.

As a reminder, the three markers of PTSD are continuously reliving the event, trying to avoid all reminders of it, and being hyper aroused or on high alert most of the time. In order to be diagnosed with PTSD, you must exhibit all three of these symptoms in one form or another.

EXPERIENCING THE TRAUMATIC EVENT REPEATEDLY

For people with PTSD, the trauma doesn't just fade into the background after a month or so, the way it does for those without the disorder. There are numerous ways in which the event keeps coming back for the traumatized person. It can be incredibly frightening as well as energy-draining to be continually reminded of what happened. This is also known as *re-experiencing*.

Though people without PTSD may re-experience the trauma, it's usually brief and occurs soon after the event. It doesn't happen to them over and over again, or months down the line, and it may not be as intense.

Flashbacks

Unlike a memory, flashbacks seem like they're happening in the current moment. It replaces the current situation that you're in. Many people can't tell that they're having a flashback while it's occurring, because it appears so real.

The emotions are the same as in the original event, and usually the sensations are as well: sounds, scents, tastes, images, and physical reactions. That's why it's so hard to tell when you're having one, because it plays out in your mind just as it did in real life.

Researchers have discovered that flashbacks tend to center on the moment when the person first realized in the initial event that they were in danger. Due to this phenomenon, someone who's currently in the middle of a flashback may suddenly start taking action, which injures them or others. They're trying to avoid a danger that's occur-ring to them *right now.*

Of course, the person suffering from PTSD doesn't mean to lash out or harm anyone else. They're reliving an event that happened in the past as if it's in the present and trying to avoid whatever the results were. Unfortunately, someone without the disorder and who's never experienced a flashback often doesn't understand what's occurring. They might believe that the one with PTSD is trying to hurt them or the people around them.

Why does this potentially harmful phenomenon occur? Your amyg-dala and hippocampus are the main sources for these repeated, intense re-experiences. The amygdala is activated in the fight-or-flight reflex, but your hippocampus is repressed by the lizard brain that wants you to survive first.

Since the amygdala is also involved with emotions, what you end up with is a strong, emotionally negative memory without a clear sequence of events because your hippocampus was offline. You've got the memories of sights, sounds, smells, etc. that are associated with the event, but no timeline or context that you'd normally get from your hippocampus.

Therefore, when you're triggered by an image, sound, or scent that's reminiscent of the event, your amygdala fires up the negative memory, senses that you're in danger, and activates the stress response.

So you're sweating, your heart speeds up, and you're breathing heavily so you can escape the hungry predator that your amygdala thinks you're facing. In fact, depending on the original trauma, you might actively try to defend yourself against it, not recognizing that you're not currently in that previous situation.

It's because your hippocampus was shut down by the stress response. If it had been functioning normally during the original event, it would provide context to the amygdala's memory. It would recognize that you're no longer in the same danger and signal your body to deactivate the stress response. But because it was offline originally, it can't provide the context that you're in a different place and time.

The amygdala doesn't receive the message that you're not in danger now, and so you're stuck with the strong negative emotion that your brain's generating (Chi, 2019).[1]

Combat veterans are known to experience flashbacks once they're in civilian life. The sound of a gunshot, or 4th of July fireworks, or even a car backfiring reminds them of the shots they heard during the war and those memories often come rushing back. The smell of fireworks can also trigger these memories.

Of course, you don't need to be a combat veteran to suffer from repeated flashbacks. I used the example of being in a car accident with a white SUV in an earlier chapter. If you witnessed an event such as a wildfire that ravaged your town, you might have flashbacks if you smell wood smoke in the air or sit close to a fireplace. Leaves crackling could bring back the crackling of flames and result in a flashback as well.

Someone who was assaulted by a person wearing a specific cologne may experience flashbacks whenever they're in a crowd and somebody else is wearing the same scent. Or by going to a store where the cologne is sprayed in the air.

You may not even be aware of what the trigger is. Maybe you were in a car accident in the middle of Gilroy, California (known for its garlic) or there was an air freshener in the car that you didn't pay any attention to.

Smelling a scent later, even if you don't remember it having a connection to your traumatic event, can trigger a flashback because your subconscious remembers it. This goes for all other memories as well: images, sounds, etc., not just smells.

Recurrent nightmares

These types of dreams are threatening and/or scary. People often have very physical reactions to their nightmares. For example, you might shout out in your sleep, or thrash around, or wake up soaked in sweat.

It's estimated that only about 5% of the population have nightmares. As you might imagine, the numbers are much higher for those with Post Traumatic Stress Disorder, as roughly 71-96% of sufferers experience nightmares (Veterans Administration, n.d.)[2] In addition, people who have experienced trauma are more likely to have more than one nightmare a week.

If you have PTSD and a co-occurring condition such as panic or anxiety disorder, you're more likely to have nightmares compared to those with a single PTSD diagnosis.

Having threatening dreams after a drama is somewhat different than a "regular" nightmare, because they seem to occur earlier in the night in different stages of sleep. If you have PTSD-related nightmares, your sleep is also affected.

You don't get as much sleep as you need, and you tend to wake up more during the night and stay awake longer when you do. You have a lot of restless leg activity as well. Not only are you not getting the amount of total sleep that's best for your health, but you're also missing out on deep sleep, also known as *slow-wave* sleep (Jain, 2014).[3]

Humans cycle through different stages every time they sleep. The first stage is really just dozing off, and it's easy to be woken up. As the night (or time asleep) goes on, future cycles may not include the first stage.

The second one is non-REM, where the body relaxes more. Deep or slow-wave, also known as delta sleep for the waves that the brain produces, is the third stage and is necessary for restorative sleep.

The final stage is REM (rapid eye movement), where brain activity picks up and vivid dreams may occur. This stage is crucial for cognitive functions like memory and learning. Getting enough deep and REM sleep is important for good health mentally and physically.

Deep or slow-wave sleep is when the body repairs muscles and helps them grow. Almost all of your growth hormone, or 95%, is released during this period of the sleep cycle (WHOOP, 2019).[4] In addition to muscle repair, this stage is thought to bolster immunity as well as creative thinking and memory.

Without enough deep sleep, it's harder for your mind and body to make necessary repairs and give yourself the rest you need.

For all trauma survivors, the dreams contain elements of the trauma itself. People diagnosed with PTSD are more likely to experience their nightmares as a replay of the event compared to trauma survivors without the diagnosis.

As an example, someone who survived an assault might dream about being powerless, being held at gunpoint, being beaten, or some other scenario that involves the frightening aspects of the ordeal. Someone with PTSD is more likely to dream of the actual event itself.

Unwanted thoughts and memories

These occur when you're not really trying to recall the event. They can occur at any time and be triggered by a variety of stimuli. Or they may have no apparent trigger at all. The thoughts may force you to revisit the event, and you could end up ruminating on the ordeal, which increases the feelings of being overwhelmed and helpless.

You might recall from earlier that the prefrontal cortex helps regulate actions, which it can do by stopping an activity that might be regretted later. In addition to stopping actions, it plays a role in stopping unwanted thoughts via the hippocampus.

This process relies on the neurochemical Gamma-aminobutyric acid (GABA), which acts to inhibit nerve cells. When the brain doesn't have enough of this neurotransmitter, its ability to stop the unwanted thoughts is much lower (University of Cambridge, 2017).[5]

One thought that often comes up for those with PTSD is "Why did it happen to me?" or "What could I have done to prevent this from happening?" In many if not most cases, there's nothing you could have done to change the outcome.

For example, someone who is being abused, sexually or otherwise, might think that it's their fault for dressing, speaking, or acting a certain way. However, the abuse is always due to the abuser themselves, not the victim. The person being abused could have been acting, dressing, and speaking normally and the abuser would have found something to critique.

In other traumas due to accident, natural disaster, etc., there's still usually nothing that you could have done differently to prevent it from happening. Unfortunately, you cannot go back in time and change it even if you could identify something that would have altered the situation.

Some people with PTSD have unwanted or intrusive thoughts more frequently than flashbacks or recurrent nightmares. They can come up differently for everyone, and many with PTSD find that this symptom is aggravated when they're under more stress than usual.

For example, an adult survivor of childhood sexual abuse may experience these thoughts and memories whenever they're being physically intimate with their spouse. But another adult survivor might experience the memories and thoughts randomly throughout the day.

Unforeseen triggers

This is troubling for many people with PTSD, because it's not always possible to prepare for triggers ahead of time or to know what they are. What is a trigger? Anything that cues up your symptoms, like the intrusive thoughts described above.

There are two types of triggers. One is internal, or things that you experience within your body. Memories, thoughts, and emotions can trigger symptoms, as can physical sensations. For example, feeling angry or abandoned, out of control or vulnerable can lead to re-experiencing the trauma. So can tense muscles, body pains, or a pounding or racing heart.

The second type is external, or things that happen outside your body. Earlier you learned that almost any feature of the ordeal can bring it back to you in terrifying detail: a scent, a sound, a taste, or an image. In addition to those, things like holidays, anniversaries, and arguments.

Something others who don't have the disorder often don't understand is that the trigger doesn't have to be related to the same trauma that the survivor experienced.

News and nowadays social media often run stories that cause re-experiencing for anyone with PTSD. A story or image about any kind of trauma can trigger someone with the disorder. For example, someone who survived an assault can be triggered by a story about someone being abused or living in a war-torn country.

The news, whether you get it online, streaming, or via social media, is tuned to emphasize the negative. Earlier we talked about the negative being part of human survival strategy on the savannah, so that we'd stay away from things that would kill us.

We still have that negative bias, and in fact studies show that when given the option, we will choose negative stories over positive ones (Stafford, 2014).[6] Even people who insist that they prefer to hear good news!

Advertisers and the media know this, of course. They know that people pay more attention to negative stories, so if they want to make money (and they do) they need to run more negative stories because that's what people want. If you have PTSD, it's probably a good idea to limit your news intake from whatever sources, which will help you avoid triggers you didn't see coming.

AVOIDING REMINDERS OF THE TRAUMATIC EVENT (AVOIDANCE)

The second group of markers for a diagnosis of Post-Traumatic Stress Disorder is the active avoidance of anything that might remind a survivor of their ordeal. Avoidance is a method for isolating from any situation or feeling that might otherwise give you a reminder. There are several ways in which someone engaging in avoidance might try to evade their memories in an attempt to cope with their distress.

Why is this a problem? Avoidance often leads to more avoidance. It tells the brain that something isn't safe. The more messages that the brain receives that the world is unsafe, the more dangerous everything feels. It can lead to a downward spiral until the survivor isn't leaving their house or talking to anyone or enjoying the things that they used to love to do.

Emotional avoidance

PTSD sufferers often try to push down or ignore all emotions, whether they're related to the trauma or not. However, "feeling the feelings" is actually a very important part of the process of recovery. Trying to avoid the feelings can make PTSD symptoms worse, or last longer, than if they're dealt with.

Ignoring emotions, whether from trauma or not, doesn't actually get rid of them. Instead, they continue to build up. And at some point, they can no longer hold it all in and the emotions explode out of them.

Sometimes people seem very calm or serene, but they'll suddenly blow up for no apparent reason. (Anyone can try to ignore their emotions, not just someone with PTSD.) That's a case study in trying to push away emotions until they can no longer be hidden away.

Emotions are like a big pot of water on the stove, boiling away. You can try to put a lid on the pot, but if there's no ability for the steam to escape, the pot will eventually just blow the lid off due to the pressure from the steam. But if you leave the lid open a bit, or there's a vent in the lid, you don't have the same problem. Feeling emotions is a way to vent all that steam and prevent it from building up.

Just as it's very hard to keep the lid on a pot that's boiling hard and producing lots of steam, it takes a lot of energy to push away feelings.

Sometimes people end up abusing substances to help them avoid feelings, or they have no time left over for family or friends or work.

When your energy is all tied up in keeping emotions at bay, you can't really handle other emotions in your daily life like frustration, and so you feel like you're constantly on edge. It's similar when you're trying to avoid thoughts or memories as well, because actively trying to push them away requires a lot of energy as well.

Intimacy avoidance

Having PTSD often makes its sufferers afraid of being enmeshed with another person. While it may seem in some ways natural to avoid intimacy after sexual assault or abuse, other kinds of trauma can also result in avoiding close connections with others. It can be made worse by attempts to self-medicate through substance abuse or being sexually promiscuous.

Sometimes those with PTSD feel that they're being engulfed in a relationship, or they develop a fear of abandonment. Either of these can result in avoiding intimacy by leaving the relationship or preferring to be isolated from others and celibate.

Another way someone with PTSD might deal with intimacy is to leave a relationship as soon as it starts to get serious or they feel engulfed in it, then immediately find another partner to avoid being abandoned.

There are some common ways that intimacy avoidance gets played out. For example, the spouse who spends all day at work and barely interacts with their partner at home. The mother who ignores her husband and concentrates on their children. Abusers can be intimacy avoidant, as can their victims or the ones who chase after them.

In addition, there are signals in behavior changes that can tell the partner of someone with PTSD that the symptoms are being aggravated. They might stop holding hands, kissing, or making other kinds of physical contact, and no longer want to do things together or talk the way they used to.

They may get overly anxious if the non-PTSD partner is late or can't be contacted, or become dependent on the partner to take care of everything for them. They could start criticizing and finding fault with their partner, or become either overly protective or afraid of their partner.

Though some of these signs may appear to be the complete opposite of another, all of these are ways that PTSD can show up differently in different people. Though not all of those with PTSD will become intimacy avoidant, it's definitely not uncommon.

This can be very difficult for the intimate partner as well, unless they learn more about the disorder and why its sufferers react in certain ways. Couples who are able to work through the distress together can even find that their bond becomes stronger than ever.

Staying away from people, places, and things

This symptom of PTSD is known as *behavioral avoidance*, in contrast to emotional avoidance which is the attempt to ignore or evade thoughts, feelings and memories of the event.

As you might guess, there's overlap between these types of avoidance. Someone who is trying not to trigger any thoughts of the event will probably try to avoid situations where they believe they're likely to re-experience the trauma.

In the previous section you learned about the various triggers that can bring back the traumatic memories, from thoughts to feelings to smells and sounds. Trying to avoid setting off these triggers often results in staying away from any type of situation where you think there's likely to be a trigger.

The 9-11 terror attacks generated PTSD for many Americans, even those who weren't geographically near the sites involved. Someone previously living in New York City might have moved away to prevent reminders of the tragedy. Or to simply avoid that area of the city.

Someone who was assaulted in a specific environment will likely try to stay out of that place and anything similar to it. For example, anyone who was assaulted in a big warehouse at work will probably try to stay away from the warehouse. They might ask for a job in the office. Or they might quit that job entirely and go work somewhere else where there's no warehouse. They might avoid big box stores which are very like warehouses.

Suppose that the warehouse involved lumber, so that the smell of cut wood was associated with the assault. That person would probably also stay away from any place with the smell of fresh-cut wood, such as a lumber yard or home store. If the warehouse played a certain kind of music, they might want to avoid any place with that music, whether it be a store, a restaurant, or anything else.

They may also want to ignore anyone that was associated with the assault, even if the other person wasn't actually involved. For example, if the survivor was speaking with a co-worker prior to the assault, in their minds the colleague is associated with the event and they'll try to stay out of the way.

As noted earlier, it's not always possible to know when the cue will happen. And since there are such a variety of ways that those with PTSD can be triggered, something that might have been OK shortly after the assault can end up being a trigger itself.

For example, suppose that pop music was playing in the background during a traumatic event. At first, the survivor simply avoids the places that remind them of the ordeal. But later they're in, say, a grocery store and they hear the pop music which triggers them. Now the grocery store may be off limits to them as well.

Remember that PTSD forms after a period of time; it doesn't happen overnight. Likewise, the cues that might set a survivor off can change over time as well.

Changing routines

In an attempt to avoid the persons, places and things as discussed above, people with PTSD may change their daily habits in order to try to prevent themselves from being triggered.

A classic example of this is someone who's been in a car accident and no longer feels safe in a car, either as a driver or as a passenger. They will now need to get around by foot, bike, scooter, or public transportation. None of these methods are faster than a car, so taking alternate forms of transportation can be very time-consuming.

Which usually means that they'll need to rearrange their day to make sure they get to work or their appointments on time. They may need to get up earlier in the morning and change the time of day they exercise and do all the other things they normally take care of in a day.

At first, changing routines may not seem like it makes that much of a difference. But depending on what you're changing, it can completely change the way you live on a day-to-day basis. You might have to drive an hour out of your way every day to avoid a specific building or area that triggers you. Some people end up changing shifts at work, which can wreak havoc on their normal routines.

Restricted range of emotions (affect)

There are a couple of different ways to talk about emotions. One is *affect*, which is "An immediately expressed and observed emotion." (Washington University, n.d.)[7] The other is mood, which is more of a sustained emotion and not necessarily expressed.

The way people show a normal or broad range of affect is to use gestures, body movements, changes in tone and facial expression. Those with restricted affect show less variability in their expressions and less intensity as well.

Imagine someone with a normal affect receiving an award. You can picture them smiling, beaming, maybe even crying tears of joy. They may stand taller once they have the award in their hands, signifying the pride they feel in themselves. In their speech, thanking others for the award, their voice changes tone, rises if they're asking a question and falls afterward. They might show their award to the audience, make big gestures as they talk, etc.

Someone with restricted affect won't display their thanks or pride in such a way. For one thing, they may not be feeling much gratitude or happiness, if any at all. They might not smile, nor speak in a way that sounds like normal conversation with changes in tone and so forth. They're unlikely to make big gestures or change posture.

This is often frustrating for a PTSD survivor's loved ones. They might plan special treats or outings and be disappointed when the survivor doesn't seem to be grateful or excited about it. It's difficult for someone who has normal affect to understand why someone would be restricted. Especially if the one with PTSD enjoyed these types of treats before the event.

Not seeing a future for themselves (foreshortened future)

How can a trauma survivor get back to a quote-unquote normal life? While their loved ones often have very specific ideas of what they should do, someone with PTSD can't necessarily see a way back. Unfortunately, their loved ones are often wrong about what will help them to heal because they don't have expertise in the disorder.

Many people with PTSD feel that no one understands them and that in a way they're cut off from society. Therefore, the usual goals such as having a house, a spouse, kids, a college or graduate degree are pretty much off the table as far as they're concerned.

They feel that their life will be cut short. The severity of this symptom can vary. Some survivors may have a milder version, where they believe that something will happen to them but they're not sure when or how.

Others may experience a more severe belief of a foreshortened future, where they are convinced they'll suffer a premature death and have a specific time frame for it.

Either way, this feeling leads to depression and isolation.

HYPERAROUSAL

This is the state of heightened anxiety that your mind and body replay when thinking about or being reminded of the trauma. Although it's no longer happening, your body responds as if it were. You learned earlier about cortisol, and another chemical that the body releases is adrenaline, or epinephrine. Adrenaline affects the immediate response to danger: your pupils dilate, blood pressure is increased, etc.

In PTSD sufferers, cortisol is low. It's meant to help regulate stress over the long term, so the lack of it can make symptoms worse. The lower level of cortisol and higher levels of epinephrine lead to a system that doesn't function properly. Those with the disorder are very sensitive to certain stimuli, so their brains overreact and continue to pump out adrenaline. Which, in turn, continues to activate the fear responses.

Those who are hyper aroused can't control their responses to certain stimuli because their baseline state of arousal has changed.

For example, suppose someone without PTSD is attending a seminar and they hear a noise at the back. They'll turn to look at the source of the noise. If the noise was caused by someone entering the room late, their arousal returns to normal as they know they have nothing to fear. They'll turn back to the presenter without thinking more about it.

If on the other hand they see someone with a gun, they'll stay aroused, because they are in the presence of danger. Their fight-or-flight reflex kicks in and they'll react appropriately. For someone with PTSD, confirming that the noise is innocuous, by seeing the latecomer, doesn't actually reduce the arousal. They can stay aroused, as if danger is present, even though the stimulus is benign.

Hyperarousal shows up in a number of different ways. These effects can feed into and off each other as well. For example, being easily startled is a sign of being hyper aroused, and it's also a signal that you're hypervigilant.

Irritability

Sometimes people refer to this as agitation. It can be intense frustration and annoyance, and even anger, maybe over the smallest things. When taken to the extreme, irritability results in violence and aggression. It's the symptom that military spouses report is the most damaging to the relationship they have with their veteran (Moore, 2015).[8]

Many people, not just those with PTSD, are irritable at times. Chronic irritability is often related to health issues, from stress and low blood sugar to diabetes and depression. You might experience physical signals along with your irritability such as an increased heart rate, breathing fast, an inability to concentrate, or sweating.

Chronic anxiety

As with many other symptoms of PTSD, everyone occasionally gets anxious. Doing something new, or preparing to speak in public, or interviewing for a job are common generators of short-term anxiety. Breathing gets faster, your heart rate speeds up, and your body prepares for the situation. Those without anxiety disorders such as PTSD return to baseline after the situation is over.

Long-term anxiety, which is common for PTSD, can be dangerous to your health because of all the stress chemicals that your brain releases on a regular basis. People who already have heart disease are at higher risk for an event such as a heart attack.

Your digestive system is also affected, which leads to stomach pain, diarrhea, nausea, and loss of appetite. As you learned earlier, a constant wash of stress chemicals such as adrenaline weakens your immune system over time, so it's easier for you to get sick. In addition, vaccines might not work as well when your immune system isn't working properly.

Anxiety often causes insomnia, depression, and headaches too. In addition, people with chronic anxiety may lose their sex drive and become fatigued during the day. Sometimes anxiety results in a panic attack, which is a feeling of extreme terror accompanied by physical symptoms.

Difficulty with falling or staying asleep

There are a variety of ways in which someone with PTSD might have issues sleeping. It might be harder to fall asleep in the first place, or they could wake up earlier than they wanted to. The disorder causes some sufferers to wake up a lot during the night and not be able to fall back asleep or take a long time to do so. As a consequence, the sleep they're able to get isn't restorative or restful.

People who aren't able to sleep at night often try to sleep during the daytime instead. Which makes it harder for them to fall asleep at night, and so on in a vicious circle. Worrying about sleep or being afraid to sleep due to potential nightmares about the trauma, make the issues worse but are very common for people with PTSD.

The edginess that comes along with hyperarousal interferes with the ability to get to or stay asleep. In addition, being so reactive to stimuli often means that the trauma survivor wakes up easily to noises or other stimuli.

Research shows that those with PTSD are more likely to have *sleep apnea* (Tull, 2020).[9] This condition results in breathing repeatedly stopping and restarting during sleep. People who snore, are overweight, smoke, drink too much or have diabetes are also at higher risk.

In the obstructive type, the muscles of the throat relax and block the airways. Central sleep apnea happens when the brain doesn't send the correct signals to the muscles, and the complex type has both these symptoms.

Doctors can test you to see if you have sleep apnea. Some of the symptoms include snoring, interrupted breathing during sleep, waking with a dry mouth, morning headaches, insomnia, and irritability.

Sleep apnea leads to a higher risk for many illnesses such as cardiovascular disease and high blood pressure. It can complicate surgery when you need an anesthetic.

Angry outbursts

Anger is a very common reaction for anyone who's been through trauma. For some survivors, the high levels of arousal that you experience may actually lead you to try to find situations that you need to be alert for to ward off danger. Others may prefer to numb the sensation with substances or other addictive behaviors.

When a person is under threat, the best response can often be an aggressive reaction. Those who experienced trauma as a child may never have learned any other way of responding, and they often act impulsively, without thinking. Other aggressive reactions include backstabbing, doing a bad job on purpose, self-blaming, and harming yourself.

One of the mental issues for trauma survivors is that they can't tell when their thoughts have been affected by the experience. They believe that they're responding to the situation in front of them, but they're still reacting to what happened.

For example, in combat it's important to follow the rules and obey the leader in order to survive. A veteran at home may lash out angrily at their spouse and family when they disobey or question the rules.

Because trauma so often involves a loss of control, many PTSD sufferers end up trying to enforce control rigidly after the situation. Because you're being inflexible, you'll likely get hostile responses from those around you. Which feeds back into your inability to trust others.

It's another vicious cycle, especially when you are horrified by your outburst and determined to keep an even tighter lid over your emotions, including your anger. Unfortunately, this will make future outbursts both inevitable and excessive.

Being able to work on your anger (which you'll discover more about later in this book) will help you avoid responding to triggers with intense or explosive anger. In turn, you'll be able to build better relationships.

Easily startled

Everyone gets startled sometimes. Horror movies activate the startle response with a "jump scare," where the monster suddenly appears, or the hero suddenly disappears (often accompanied by ominous music on the soundtrack.) For most people, the event has to be higher stress in order for the startle reflex to kick in.

Someone with PTSD has an extreme or excessive startle response, where they overreact to something that happens suddenly. The strong response to a mild stressor (that doesn't affect people without the disorder) can happen at any time to a sufferer, whether the environment is like the traumatic one or not.

The exaggerated startle response, as you might imagine, is linked to the stress and fear responses. A stress hormone known as CRF[10] makes your amygdala more sensitive to the neurochemical norepinephrine, which triggers the stress response. This link between CRF and norepinephrine is also involved in areas of the brain that get involved with drug abuse, which may be why people with PTSD are also at higher risk for alcoholism.

You might refer to yourself as "jumpy" when you have the excessive startle response. A slight noise behind you could cause you to whirl around and be ready to fight or flee, whereas the same noise for someone else doesn't register as a threat.

Involuntarily trying to cover the back of your neck or your throat, parts of your body that are vulnerable, is a reflexive way to react to being startled. In addition to experiencing this more often, you might also feel more distress after a startling experience.

For example, most people watching a horror movie will settle back down after a jump scare, or even laugh at themselves for having the reaction. But someone with PTSD might be genuinely upset and unable to go back to watching the movie for some period of time.

Constantly on the lookout for threats (hypervigilant)

This isn't just being extra vigilant. It's more extreme than that. People who are hypervigilant are often exhausted because they are constantly scanning for threats. Hypervigilance interferes with their ability to function in daily life.

You know you're suffering from hypervigilance if you're experiencing one or more of the following signs:

1. Overestimating potential threats

You're on the lookout for things that are either unlikely to happen or exaggerated. For example, you might find yourself insisting on a seat in the restaurant with your back to the wall so that you can see everything happening around you and no one can sneak behind you. Is it likely that you're in danger in the restaurant? Unless you're a Mob boss, not really. Similarly, you may insist on remaining near the exits in a store, restaurant, movie theatre, etc. Although it's highly unlikely that anything will happen to you, your state of hyper-arousal prevents you from assessing risk in a logical way.

2. Avoiding perceived threats

You may also find yourself trying to avoid any place that might be perilous, even if there's no current threat. For example, you might skip any kind of public gathering, even if it's for something as innocent as watching the lighting of the town's Christmas tree. Or for something that you previously enjoyed, such as an outdoor concert.

In the extreme, this manifests as agoraphobia, where you don't want to be anywhere you perceive as being difficult to escape. People in this condition rarely leave their homes because calculating escape routes from new or unfamiliar places can be too taxing.

3. Increased startle reflex as discussed above

4. Sustained adrenaline response

> When there's no threat to be seen, you're still experiencing the symptoms associated with adrenaline release: dilated pupils, fast heartbeat, and so on. This was explained in the example under Hyperarousal when someone with PTSD in a seminar can turn to see that a noise was due to a latecomer, but several minutes later their heart is still racing and they're breathing fast.

When people are hypervigilant, they can enter into a state of paranoia where they feel that they need to arm themselves, whether the weapons are legal or not. Or they may decide extra locks for doors and windows are needed, or that a sophisticated (and expensive) alarm system is necessary, or even install a panic room to escape to when something goes wrong.

PTSD DIAGNOSIS

In order for a person to be officially diagnosed with Post-Traumatic Stress Disorder, they must have at least one reaction or symptom from each of the three categories. In other words, you need to experience hyperarousal, avoidance, and re-experiencing the trauma. You may have one symptom in one area and multiples in the other two areas, but you must have at least one in each category to be diagnosed.

As a reminder, re-experiencing may occur through recurrent nightmares, flashbacks, intrusive or unwanted thoughts and memories, and unforeseen triggers. Avoidance can be emotional, intimacy, and behavioral. Symptoms can include not touching or interacting with a partner, shutting down emotions, changing routines, exhibiting a restricted range of emotions, and seeing only a foreshortened future.

Hyperarousal can manifest in a variety of ways. You may feel irritable, have chronic anxiety and sleep issues, have episodes of explosive anger, be easily startled and hypervigilant.

While some of these symptoms at the mild or moderate end are common for humanity in general, experiencing them intensely or for a prolonged period of time may indicate the presence of PTSD.

CHAPTER SUMMARY

There are three categories of symptoms that comprise a diagnosis of PTSD, and they're also a part of the C-PTSD diagnosis. The trauma survivor needs to present at least one behavior or symptom in each category to be classified under Post-Traumatic Stress Disorder. These symptoms also must last longer than a month for the diagnosis because those without the disorder often undergo the same symptoms, but theirs resolves in about a month.

- People with PTSD continue to re-experience their trauma as if it were currently happening, which often results in excessive reactions to the existing situation which can be violent.

- Those with the disorder try to stay away from anything associated with the trauma, which is known as avoidance and includes the pushing away of emotions.
- Someone with Post-Traumatic Stress Disorder experiences hyperarousal, where their brains are very reactive to even mild stimuli and continuously releasing stress and fear chemicals.
- While mild or short-duration episodes of many of these signs are experienced by a lot of people, not all of whom have an anxiety disorder, the intense and long-lasting characteristics of the symptoms are key for PTSD sufferers.

In the next chapter you will learn about affect dysregulation, which is one of the key markers for C-PTSD.

4

AFFECT DYSREGULATION

Now that you understand the various symptoms that manifest for trauma survivors who have PTSD, you'll learn about the additional symptoms that mark sufferers of C-PTSD. "Affect dysregulation" may sound like a very complex term, but recall that *affect* just refers to the expression of emotion. *Dysregulation* is similar to dysfunction, meaning that something isn't being regulated properly. More simply, we'll be discussing emotions that aren't properly regulated. People with C-PTSD are incapable or impaired when it comes to controlling emotions, or the expression of them.

WHY EMOTIONAL CONTROL AND REGULATION IS SO IMPORTANT

You might be wondering why not having control over your emotions is so crucial to your functioning that the inability to do so is a symptom of C-PTSD. You might be asking yourself, "What's the big deal if I lose control once in a while and explode or yell at my family?"

In fact, there's not really much anyone can do to control their emotions. You might recall from earlier chapters that emotions are automatically generated, so it's not possible to simply stop anger from appearing, or frustration or sadness. However, you can control your actions. If you can regulate your emotions, you control how and when you express them. People with good emotional control rarely lash out at others, even when they're feeling angry or disappointed. They also don't lash out at themselves, or turn the anger inward, which can result in depression and self-harm.

You've probably heard of IQ or intelligence quotient, which basically measures how well people can perform logic and reasoning tasks. It's considered to be pretty much fixed at birth. But you may not have heard of EQ, which stands for emotional intelligence, and can be developed and improved over time. It refers to how well a person can manage their own emotions and help others with theirs.

Having a high EQ is necessary for strong relationships, because those who have a lot of emotional intelligence understand what's going on with others as well as themselves in a nonjudgmental way. They're able to communicate well with others and build the bonds that we humans need to feel good and be happy with our lives.

It's also a growing need in the business and leadership world, because the old command-and-control style of leadership, at least for civilians, has largely been discarded in favor of a style where leaders inspire their followers instead of ordering them around.

There are four or five requirements for EQ, depending on who you ask, and emotional regulation is one of them. Without being in control of your emotions, your emotional intelligence will be poor. That affects your home life, your work life, and everything in between.

1. Self-awareness

This trait means that you are aware of your emotions, and also how they are affecting you and those around you. You're aware of how your actions affect you and others too. you're not trying to push away your feelings, or pretend that they don't exist, because they do.

Self-aware people understand when their feelings are affecting them. For example, they know when they're sad or angry, and ask for a time-out or a delay if someone wants them to make a decision. They're able to recognize when a strong emotion might prevent them from taking the right action, and give themselves some time to sort it out first.

They're also knowledgeable about their own strengths and weaknesses. Sometimes it's hard for trauma survivors to remember that they have strengths, especially when they're feeling overwhelmed and out of control. Yet everyone has something that they're good at or a good quality to them, like kindness or compassion. Or being physically strong in some areas, or intelligent, or having a creative mind or an artist's eye.

Self-aware people also understand where they're weak. They may choose to try to improve in these areas, or they might ask for help from someone they know is strong in that area.

For example, people who aren't good at numbers or money can ask their friends and family who are strong in these areas to help them make sure they're on a good financial footing. They know that they can help others who are struggling in areas where they're strong, and that everyone has some of both.

You also know what your own values are. What's most important to you? Supporting your family? Being honest? Caring for those less fortunate? Staying humble and right-sized, where you neither puff yourself up nor put yourself down?

2. Self-regulation

This is all about staying in control of your actions. Feelings and thoughts come up in the human brain all the time, but that doesn't mean they must be acted upon. They're not always true or based in reality, so reacting to them without pausing or thinking can often lead to the wrong decisions.

Interestingly, being in control means that you're more aware of your emotions, not less. That way you can evaluate the likelihood that the feeling you're experiencing is likely to help you or harm you. When you're so numb to what's going on within you and don't understand the emotions that are occurring, whether you acknowledge them or not, you have no way of knowing how they're impacting your actions.

By contrast, when you know that you're angry, you also know that you're more likely to lash out at your family members even over small stresses that really don't matter in the grand scheme of things. So, before you open your mouth, you can consider whether what's about to come out is going to be beneficial or not. And if not, implement some strategies to help you cool down instead. (You'll learn about these strategies later in this book.)

By being in control, you can act according to your values. If one of your values is prioritizing your family and you're able to self-regulate, you stop lashing out at them over small details.

You also give yourself time to make good decisions based on the actual facts of the situation at hand, and not look at the circumstances through the lens of your emotions. And you'll be able to hold yourself accountable and stop blaming others when things go wrong.

This is invaluable at work. No manager wants to put up with a worker who's constantly blaming others for their errors. They prefer employees who can own up to their mistakes, which means they can learn from them and prevent similar errors in the future.

3. Motivation

Being able to pursue your goals is also critical for the emotionally intelligent. You don't need someone standing over you telling you what to do all day, which most of us find annoying anyway!

Motivated people also want to do good work and get the job done right. It's actually easier to get it right the first time, because having to correct mistakes results in more work.

4. Empathy

Building those important bonds with other people requires you to be able to step into their shoes and see things from their perspective. When you're busy trying to ignore or push away inconvenient emotions, you really have no emotional space to spare to think about other people.

Just like you, people want to be seen and heard. Listening to them and understanding their feelings is key to this. But how can you understand someone else's feelings when you can't understand your own?

5. Social skills

Being able to communicate well with others is important in all aspects of life: family, romance, work, even going to the grocery store. People who have good social skills are able to manage conflicts in their own relationships.

They know how to praise others, and they can accept negative feedback and use it as an opportunity to learn, rather than feeling attacked.

Plus, when you're able to be vulnerable, others can be vulnerable too. That helps you connect with others. No one can really build a bond with someone whose surface appears to be perfect and shiny. When you let others in, they feel they can bond with you and relate to you.

Earlier we talked about emotions as being like a pot of boiling water, and trying to cover it with a lid simply means all the pressure builds and the lid eventually blows off. When you're in control, your emotions may be boiling, but you're actually not trying to fit a tight lid on the pot.

When you can regulate properly, you're able to tweak the flame underneath the pot so that the water doesn't boil over. You're controlling the source, so you affect how much power the boiling water has.

You can turn down the flame so there's not as much steam coming out, instead of trying to suppress it by covering it up.

The ability to regulate how you express yourself is key. When you avoid feeling your emotions, there's no way that you can control them or understand how they affect you and the others around you. Only someone who acknowledges their emotions will be able to regulate them. Affect dysregulation prevents you from understanding, acknowledging, and regulating how you behave.

Bear in mind that regulation does not mean ignoring your feelings. When you can regulate them appropriately, you are aware when they come up for you, but you don't necessarily act on them. You have the emotional ability to adjust the flame or soothe yourself, instead of allowing the water to boil out of control.

HOW DO YOU LEARN SELF-REGULATION?

The ability to control how you express your emotions is not an innate ability of humankind. Typically, those who are strong in this skill learn it from their parents or caregivers.

If you've ever been in close contact with a baby, you know that they are incapable of soothing themselves. They cry when they're wet, when they're in pain, when they're hungry, or when they want something. They can't stop themselves crying, so the parent has to change them, feed them, rock them, give them a pacifier, or whatever the baby needs at that moment.

As babies grow into infants and then children, they learn more skills to help them cope. You might see a young child sucking their thumb, which is a method of self-soothing. Their parents, teachers, and others around them can help them continue to grow and mature.

Having a nurturing environment is key for learning how to cope with emotions. A child who grows up in a healthy way learns that they can ask for help and get it. They discover that they can be comforted by others when they face challenges, and also how they can comfort themselves. A nurturing caregiver teaches them how to think about puzzles and problems to solve them rather than being overwhelmed.

A child who doesn't grow up with nurturing parents or caregivers don't learn these skills. Instead, they may learn that there is no help available when they ask, and they'll stop asking. They are not able to find comfort in others or in themselves, which teaches them that the world is not a safe place and other people can't be trusted.

Due to these issues, childhood abuse, maltreatment, or neglect is a common factor in those who have been diagnosed with C-PTSD and is known to cause affect dysregulation (Franco, 2018).[1] It's also possible for trauma to be transmitted from the parent to the child, because trauma survivors who struggle with their own coping skills cannot help their children develop in a healthy way.

WHAT IS AFFECT DYSREGULATION?

Also known as emotion dysregulation, it's the inability to deal with emotions such as sadness, anger, or fear. You can't always control either the intensity of the feelings, or how long they stay with you.

Rationally, you might be aware that you need to shake it off in order to move on, or to have a healthier relationship, but the emotion stays with you instead. The effects of having the feelings remain for a long period of time can be very intense.

The inability to deal with emotions is another aspect of your brain trying to protect you. In order to prevent the uncomfortable feelings from appearing, all emotion gets shut down. It affects memory as well, which is the reason many sufferers don't remember the event(s) later.

For example, suppose that you end up having an argument with your brother about something, large or small. When you think about where the fight fits into your life, it's nothing that can't be solved or maybe even brushed off. But you're unable to let it go.

Thinking about the argument might prevent you from sleeping at night. Or you can't stop thinking about it while you're at work, which causes you to make silly mistakes that you'd normally avoid. You might even be telling yourself to stop thinking about it, or shake it off, or move on. But you can't.

This seeps into your interactions with him when you have a family picnic or outing. You might get to the point where you keep escalating until the two of you end up shouting unforgivable things to each other, and end up damaging the relationship badly, possibly beyond repair.

Or you're desperate not to let that happen, so instead you choose to numb yourself. Maybe you start drinking too much. Or you decide to numb out by hitting the casino or heading to the mall to shop 'til you drop. You might be thinking that you cause less harm this way.

Unfortunately, even if you believe you're only hurting yourself, usually you're still affecting the whole family. When you're drunk or high most of the time, you're unable to truly participate in family life because you're not really there even if you're physically present.

Or you're physically absent, plus you're spending so much money that eventually you're drowning in debt. You could easily end up at the point where you can't pay for your basic necessities, such as heat or electricity or a roof over your head.

There are a number of symptoms that point to someone who is suffering from affect dysregulation. Some of these are also involved in the categories of PTSD (avoidance and hyperarousal) and they can also feed off each other. You've already learned about a few of these symptoms in earlier chapters, so the details are not repeated here.

- Depression
- Anxiety
- Excessive shame and anger

Shame is the sense of being worthless, small, or powerless in a situation. It's usually a reflection of feeling that other people are looking at you negatively, with disgust or disdain. That doesn't necessarily mean that the person who feels shame is actually worthless or a subject of disdain, but they believe they are.

Shame produces physical changes in the body as well. It's often accompanied by a sense of time having slowed down, so that the feeling of shame is actually magnified. People feeling shame also experience an increased heart rate, and sometimes sweating and/or blushing as well.

The brain sees shame as a threat, probably an interpersonal danger, and activates the fight-or-flight reflex as a response (Traumatic Stress Institute, 2007).[2] Because feelings of shame are disorganized and often intense, the shame isn't precisely encoded in the memory. It can spread and be connected to other memories that didn't originally have shame attached to them.

It shows up in speech typically as a barely audible voice that speaks with a lot of pauses and repetition, and the listener often can't make out the words.

Traumatic events often lead to shame for their survivors. The trauma makes them feel helpless or powerless, which in turn they feel makes them weak or ineffective. These feelings are associated with a sense of shame.

- Self-harm
- Sexual promiscuity or other excessive sexual behavior

These behaviors are another way to avoid uncomfortable feelings or push the trauma away. It's common, especially for those who developed C-PTSD as a result of sexual violence or abuse. However, even those with a different trauma use sex as a way to numb out or try to ignore their emotions.

Eating disorders

Like many of the other symptoms of affect dysregulation, eating disorders are a way to respond to the powerlessness and helplessness induced by a traumatic event. Starving yourself or making sure that you eliminate calories in some way (such as purging) are ways to assert control over yourself.

Another reason eating disorders are often an issue for C-PTSD sufferers is that they're a common reaction to rape and other sexual abuse. Although the exact mechanism isn't yet known, the association of eating disorders and sexual trauma is well-documented (Hower, 2018).[3]

Substance abuse

Whether the drug of choice is legal (alcohol, prescription medication, and marijuana in some locations) or illegal, overusing drugs to numb the uncomfortable feelings is a well-known, if unhealthy, coping mechanism.

It provides temporary relief, but once the effect wears away, the user is no better off. This often leads to escalating use in an attempt to stay self-medicated at all times. With some substances, the reward system of the brain is altered, and you need higher and higher amounts of the drug to be able to stop feeling your feelings.

Excessive perfectionism

Like eating disorders, an unhealthy level of perfectionism is a way for survivors of traumatic events to take back control of their lives. There are people who are naturally disposed towards perfectionism. Trying to do your best at all times is not necessarily a bad thing.

Everyone makes mistakes, so the healthy response is to learn from it and move on. But for C-PTSD sufferers, the need to achieve the goals is intense and failure to meet them is grounds for self-loathing and criticism. They see errors or less than 100% as a character flaw, not as a steppingstone for improvement.

When you spend a long time in a situation where every mistake can lead to severe consequences and everything you do is criticized, the natural result is a fear of failure. Excessive perfectionism is a way to try to evade conflict and punishment.

Some signs that you're experiencing perfectionism to an extreme level include:

- Expecting more from yourself than you would from someone else in the same situation
- Expecting others to give you negative feedback even when you've exceeded
- Taking so much time over your work that you put off fun and interesting hobbies or activities
- Rechecking your work over and over
- Stressing out about whether a routine task is done to perfection
- Over-performing to the extent that you realize later you didn't need to do so much work.
- High levels of interpersonal conflict

Complex trauma often results in a survivor who is both afraid to trust others and have relationships, as well as fear of being rejected or criticized. It's very hard to build or maintain bonds with other people when you have these fears, which leads to a lot of conflict.

You might be arguing with parents, siblings, your own children, your spouse, friends, colleagues, or anyone who crosses your path. An overstimulated fear response prevents you from giving other people the benefit of the doubt and to hear criticism and/or rejection when none is intended.

Suicidal thoughts and attempts

Suicide may be another way of exerting control for someone who previously felt powerless. Suicidal ideation happens when you often think about committing suicide, how you would do it, possibly role-play various scenarios and test them out.

There are a variety of ways that emotional dysregulation shows up in ordinary life. They're often characterized by outbursts that are out of proportion to the circumstances. Suppose that your partner cancels a date because they're not feeling well. Someone with good self-regulation would be disappointed, but then move on to call a friend to hang out or watch a movie. They'd shake off the feeling of being disappointed or rejected because it's just one date.

However, someone with C-PTSD is more likely to assume that means the partner doesn't love them anymore and start crying and eating ice cream. Or cut or burn themselves, consider suicide, or retreat to the bottle. Because they're constantly in a state of high arousal, these types of events seem much more momentous and threatening than they do for someone who doesn't have that elevated response.

Or consider a scenario where you're at the post office and they don't have the package for you to pick up as they should and ask you to come back the next day. A regulated response would be to feel the disappointment but recognize that this kind of thing happens and go on about their day. But someone with affect dysregulation is more likely to start shouting at the clerk and throw a pen at them.

The signs can be more subtle than that. Survivors of complex trauma often believe that they don't belong in a given situation. Everyone else seems to be having a great time and you might be feeling alone and unwanted. Maybe you're at the company holiday party and everyone else seems to know everybody there and having a lot of fun. Meanwhile, you feel like you don't belong there and when you go home, you binge on food or drugs.

UNDER-REGULATION OF AFFECT

There are two ways in which affect dysregulation can present: in over-regulation and under-regulation. A DESNOS diagnosis (per the DSM-V) refers to under-regulation as an alteration in regulation of affect and impulse.

When affect is under-regulated, the C-PTSD sufferer loses control over their emotions and expresses them in an intense manner, overwhelming their ability to reason through the situation. There are two ways in which trauma survivors demonstrate their under-regulation. One is through extreme emotional distress such as fear and rage. The other is behavioral, resulting in impulsive and aggressive actions.

This is a well-known consequence of childhood trauma especially. If the infant's caregiver isn't available to help soothe high arousal states, the intense negative experience requires all the child's mental and emotional resources to withstand the dysregulation. The combination of the trauma and the lack of caregiver response prevent the child from learning how to manage the various levels of arousal.

When your emotions are under-regulated, you don't have good coping skills to deal with uncomfortable feelings and you're not able to self-soothe. The above example of losing control in the post office is an under-regulation experience. You can't manage the feeling of disappointment or control your actions over it, and you fly into a rage even though the situation doesn't call for it.

It's not just anger that people with under-regulation struggle with. Fear or anxiety can bloom into full-fledged terror out of proportion to the trigger. Consider going to a "haunted house" around Halloween that's been designed to induce a few scares. They normally have spooky music, some monsters that suddenly pop up in front of you, and other jump scares like you might see in a horror movie.

Someone without the disorder might experience fear when a scaly hand suddenly reaches out for them from behind a curtain, but once they realize it's just a part of the attraction, they can relax, and the fear dissipates. But if you have C-PTSD, something like that could very well trigger a panic attack or other manifestation of extreme terror that leaves you unable to function normally.

For those with C-PTSD, impulsive behaviors like bulimia and binge-shopping are often an attempt to distract themselves from the negative emotions. They're more likely than other people to act impulsively when they're experiencing feelings like sadness or anger, whereas people without the disorder who simply have a tendency to act without thinking do so no matter what they're feeling.

The short-term reward of the impulse also counters or distracts from the feelings that the survivor doesn't want to accept or think about. For example, when you cut yourself deliberately the physical pain can make you feel better, at least briefly, and prevent you from experiencing the negative emotion or thinking about the trauma.

When it comes to aggression, there are two types of aggression that people can have, whether or not they've survived a trauma. One is *impulse aggression*, which is pretty much what it sounds like - emotional and reactive. This type is uncontrolled or spontaneous. The second is *premeditated aggression*, in which the reaction is planned and controlled. People can be both.

Combat veterans with PTSD show signs of impulse aggression, but not usually the premeditated type. Which makes sense, since in this kind of affect dysregulation emotions are uncontrollable. However, women with trauma backgrounds demonstrate both kinds of aggression (Miles, et al, 2017).[4]

What does aggression look like? It's an act of hostility that can do damage to another person (though you can also be aggressive toward yourself.) It's behind a range of behaviors from verbal abuse all the way to violence. However, aggression is often a defense reaction and isn't always meant to hurt someone else, especially when it's impulsive. If in the post office example, you attacked the clerk verbally, that's an aggressive act too.

There are four types of aggression, and women and men are equally aggressive. However, women are more likely to use indirect or verbal forms (Good Therapy, 2019).[5]

1. Accidental

This kind of aggression is not meant to cause anyone harm, and it's often just the consequence of being careless. For example, if you're running for the bus, you might accidentally bump into someone else who's standing on the sidewalk.

2. Expressive

This type is intentional, but it's still not meant to hurt anyone. In the post office example, throwing a pen across the table is intentional but there's no real intent to injure the clerk.

3. Hostile

Someone in the throes of hostile aggression means to inflict pain, whether it's emotional or physical. Malicious gossip is hostile, as is bullying. Also, reacting aggressively when provoked is also hostile. Verbally abusing the post office clerk is clearly hostile.

4. Instrumental

This type comes from a conflict over things or what someone perceives as their right. Suppose that you have a parking space at work that you think of as yours, because you always park there, even though it's not specifically assigned to you. If one day a coworker parks in "your" space, you might respond by starting a nasty rumor about them or "accidentally" bumping into them in the hallway.

OVER-REGULATION OF AFFECT

In contrast with under-regulation, those who over-regulate try to ignore and shut down their emotions. They don't want to acknowledge when the feelings occur or deal with them in any way. Over time, they're often less able to determine when they're experiencing emotions and what the emotions actually are. They shut down so they don't have to re-experience the feelings and the trauma that occurred.

DESNOS also includes alterations in attention or consciousness in the list of symptoms, which is known as over-regulation. These changes can include both amnesia and dissociative episodes. There's a variety of ways in which C-PTSD sufferers might experience dissociation, which is when you feel detached from things.

It's not something that you transition to automatically after your fight-or-flight reflex is activated, but rather it's something that happens over time. It's another way in which your brain is trying to protect you from the trauma. The more you feel disconnected, the more you dissociate.

On the mild side, the interruptions in consciousness which is the foundation of dissociation result in daydreaming or briefly "spacing out." More severe reactions include feeling disconnected from your body or the processes of your body.

One type of dissociation is known as *depersonalization*, which is a detachment from your identity or yourself. For example, you might have an "out of body" sensation where you feel like you're floating away from your body, or watching it do things as if you're watching a movie.

Or your body may seem like it's no longer yours, and you're wondering why you're attached to it. Maybe you no longer recognize yourself in the mirror, or you have to keep checking the mirror to make sure there's a reflection so you can satisfy yourself that you are real.

You might have the sense when you talk that it's not really "you," but a robot or something that's not you is in control. Other symptoms include feeling like parts of your body are much larger or much smaller than they actually are.

You might not feel "real," which is an aspect of dissociation known as *derealization*. Sometimes people experience this when they feel that real life is actually a dream, because everything around them (and possibly themselves) doesn't appear to be real. Or you might feel disconnected from loved ones, like there's a glass wall between you. You can see them, but you can't reach them, and they can't reach you.

Your surroundings might seem blurry or colorless or fake, like it's a stage or movie set. Conversely, some people have a very sharp awareness of what's around them and everything seems very clear and high-definition.

Derealization is often accompanied by distortions in space and time. Something that happened relatively recently seems like it was years ago. Or objects in your surroundings seem either much farther away or much closer than they actually are.

With dissociation you can lose time as well. The missing time can be a few minutes, to a few days, to large chunks of your childhood.

In the most severe cases, you might switch between different states of self, also known as "alters." This is usually diagnosed as Dissociative Identity Disorder, which you may have heard referred to as Multiple Personality Disorder.

When you continue to dissociate over a longer period of time, you may develop amnesia as well. This might show up as an inability to feel certain emotions, because you've left behind the ability to feel. Or you may experience it as not remembering what happened to you, or both. The memory of what happened is not gone completely, but your brain is shifting focus to things that you can better handle.

But just as you need to feel your emotions in order to recover, at some point you need to remember what happened to you so that you can deal with it. The amnesia is both a method of coping as well as an obstacle on the way to recovery.

To someone who's never experienced dissociative amnesia, the idea that you could actually forget a serious trauma may seem ludicrous. Yet it happened to a childhood friend of mine, whom I'll call Rhonda. I didn't know when we were growing up, as most outside a family don't know, that she was being sex trafficked by her mother and step-father. For all outward appearances, she belonged to a normal suburban family and led a normal suburban life.

Her family moved overseas in high school and for a while we lost touch. The trafficking continued until she was in college, and in adulthood she didn't remember any of this had happened. Then she married and had children, and with the children came the flashbacks and other symptoms. Fortunately, she was able to find a therapist who could help her work through the trauma and help her protect her own children.

As with many of the other symptoms of C-PTSD, dissociation doesn't just happen to those with a type of anxiety disorder. Everyone daydreams sometimes, which is actually positive for the brain and helps you be more creative. Similarly, "spacing out" briefly is a pretty common occurrence.

Many people experience a fleeting feeling of being outside their bodies, or that their surroundings are dreamlike instead of real. However, for someone without the disorder, these episodes are typically fleeting and rare.

For sufferers of C-PTSD, however, these sensations interfere with their ability to live their life normally. They may keep coming back; they're often very distressing; and they can't be shaken off.

CHAPTER SUMMARY

Affect dysregulation is a part of Complex Post-Traumatic Stress Disorder, because sufferers for a variety of reasons are not able to regulate themselves emotionally.

- Emotional regulation is a key factor in emotional

intelligence, which is an important component of life and work in the 21st century.

- Humans are not born with the ability to regulate their emotions but learn it from healthy parents and other authority figures.
- Those whose parents don't self-regulate typically don't learn these skills either, and instead they're subject to affect dysregulation or the inability to manage emotions appropriately.
- There are a number of signs that someone is dealing with affect dysregulation, which can range from depression and self-harm to excessive perfectionism and a lot of interpersonal conflict.
- One type of dysregulation is known as under-regulation, which is demonstrated by aggression or lack of impulse control.
- The other type is over-regulation, where the survivor tries to shut off the feelings, and may end up dissociating from themselves or their surroundings or experiencing amnesia.

In the next chapter you will learn about another symptom of C-PTSD, which is negative self-concept.

5

NEGATIVE SELF-CONCEPT

It's true that nearly everyone on the planet feels badly about themselves from time to time. Not getting the date, or the job promotion, or muffing a presentation in front of the boss: all of these happen and cause some negative thoughts and self-talk. But for trauma survivors, the negative self-concept runs much deeper than the occasional sense of disappointment or that you should have tried harder.

It's the lens through which you view everything that happens in the world, as a reflection of your own bad, weak, powerless, ineffective, shameful, self. What recovery includes is the realization that these things you've been telling yourself, or that you believe about yourself, are not true. It's the trauma speaking, and your brain's attempt to make sense of it.

WHAT IS SELF-CONCEPT?

It's the way that any one person evaluates, perceives, or thinks about themselves. It begins taking shape in infancy, with the realization that you're separate from other people and you're yourself all the time. This *existential self* is the most basic aspect of selfhood, and recognition starts as soon as you're two or three months old (Mcleod, 2008).[1]

You smile, and your caregiver smiles back. You touch the mobile in your crib, and it moves. Babies begin this fundamental aspect of self in relation to their surroundings, both people and things.

Next comes the awareness of the *categorical self*, where you see that you're also an object in the world, just as your crib mobile is, and you become aware of yourself and the properties that you have, or how you can be categorized.

Age and gender are usually the first two categories to be applied, as you discover that you're two years old and you're a girl. In young childhood, the categories are concrete instead of abstract: age, gender, height, hair color, favorite toys. As people grow older, they start adding the more abstract characterizations to their sense of self: introversion, animal-lover, enjoys working with their hands, etc.

There are three components to the self-concept of humans (Ibid).[2]

1. Self-image

This is how you view yourself. And it may not reflect reality, especially for trauma survivors. It's influenced by a variety of factors, such as parents, friends, colleagues, media, social media, teachers, supervisors, etc.

All these factors have a varying degree of impact. Parents, especially in early childhood, have a great deal to do with your self-image. Caregivers who treat their children well and support them are more likely to raise kids who have more of a positive self-image, compared to parents who neglect or abuse their children.

"Who am I?" is a basic question of self-image, and the responses tend to come back in one of two ways. One is social roles, or a response of "I'm a teacher," "I'm a son," and so forth. The other group is personality traits, such as "I love animals" or "I have a sense of humor" or "I'm impatient."

People also describe themselves in terms of physical characteristics like height, hair and eye color and also in the abstract, such as "I'm a child of the universe." When they're younger, the descriptions are more likely to be personality-related, whereas the older folks usually respond in terms of social role.

2. Your value

This is also known as self-esteem or self-worth. It's your measure of how valuable you are in the world.

Those with positive self-esteem tend to be more confident, optimistic, self-accepting, and less concerned with what others think about them. Telling people that they're good enough actually isn't much of an esteem-builder, whereas mastering things and becoming more competent in some areas does help increase a person's sense of self-worth.

You can probably guess how people with low self-esteem feel about themselves. They're more likely to lack self-confidence, be pessimistic, want to be someone (or anyone) else, and worry about what others think of them.

In addition to the influence of parents and caregivers, there are four factors that affect self-esteem.

3. How others react to us

When people seem to want to be around us, or are asking for our opinions, listen and agree with us, that usually makes us feel worthy. By contrast, if they avoid, ignore, or talk over us, that leads to lower self-esteem.

There can be something of a vicious circle here for someone who's feeling alienated or alone. They're less likely to approach others or to seem approachable, so other people tend to leave them alone. Which in turn makes them feel even more isolated.

4. How we compare ourselves to others

If our "target group" for comparison is richer, better-looking, more confident, etc., then we're more likely to have lower self-esteem. In contrast, when the reference group is doing worse than we are, that's positive for self-worth.

Social media has exacerbated this issue. What most people post on their feeds are carefully curated images of themselves at their best. In the holiday photo, all the kids are smiling, and the dog is lying down quietly. The vacation spot is gorgeous and dreamy. Or the business-woman carries a "statement" handbag and is wearing a gorgeous designer outfit.

Of course, people sitting in front of the computer (or phone) in their pajamas with unwashed hair will feel bad by comparison. It's important to realize that those snapshots are just those: snapshots. They're not indicative of real life either.

That holiday photo is the one out of 100 shots taken, because in all the others the youngest kid is trying to run away and the older two are hitting each other while the dog is trying to eat candy out of some-one's pocket.

The lush vacation spot is packed with mosquitos and the travelers came back coated in calamine lotion. They just decided not to capture that bit on camera. The businesswoman is carrying a fake designer purse that she picked up from a street vendor and rented the designer outfit for the photo shoot. Don't get too carried away by the perfec-tion on social media because it's artificial anyway.

5. Social roles

Let's face it, some roles carry more social sparkle than others. People look up to airline pilots, medical doctors, senators, TV anchors and the like. By contrast, no one wants to admit they're unemployed, work at a low paying job, or were in prison or a mental hospital.

When you inhabit a role that people look up to, you probably have higher self-esteem compared to someone in one of the roles that isn't seen as desirable.

6. Identification

We tend to identify with the careers that we have and our titles, as well as our roles in life and our groups. That's why many successful people have a hard time transitioning into retirement, because they no longer perceive themselves as having the "successful businessperson" identity.

Sometimes people have C-PTSD and aren't diagnosed right away. They may go years thinking that they're "crazy" because of all the symptoms discussed so far in this book. They may believe that their role is the one of "crazy aunt" or "alcoholic sister" or "black sheep of the family." They see their very identity as a person as a negative.

7. Ideal self

This is the person you want to be. For most people, whether or not they've experienced trauma or been diagnosed with a disorder, there's a gap between their self-image, or how they view themselves, and who they really want to be. (Unless you're Dolly Parton, in which case you are your ideal self.)

In many cases, the greater the gap or *incongruence* between the self-image and ideal self, the less worthy they feel. The closer a person can approach their ideal, or even if they feel like they're working to get closer, the more self-esteem they'll have.

Everyone experiences some incongruence because no one ever really lives up to their ideal selves. In order for there to be *congruence*, or significant overlap, between the actual self and the ideal self, the person must have a high positive regard for themselves.

But for those with C-PTSD, there's often not much overlap at all because their self-concept is very negative.

NEGATIVE SELF-CONCEPT

This is very common for anyone with C-PTSD, because they often feel helpless, guilty or ashamed. They may believe that they're at least partly, if not wholly, to blame for their trauma. And it follows logically that if something so bad happened to them and it was at least partially their fault, then they must be a bad person.

It's not true that a trauma survivor is a bad person, but you can see how these kinds of negative beliefs can lead to that conclusion. Many survivors feel that they're isolated and alien from other people. Especially since everyone else seems like they're functioning OK in daily life and survivors aren't.

In social interactions, people express how they feel or think about you, even in childhood. When you're picked last for the baseball team, your peers are telling you that they think you're a bad athlete. If your parents are always criticizing your grades, they may be telling you that you're dumb, or they might see you as lazy since you could have got a better grade if you tried. If your teacher praises the stories you write in English class, he's telling you that you're a good writer.

Not all of these expressions are necessarily true. You might be a great swimmer or track runner, but your hand-eye coordination is too poor for you to be good at baseball. Your parents may have received bad grades themselves and want you to do better than they did.

Comparing yourself to others and allowing them to influence how you think about yourself is natural, but it can make you think more negatively about yourself than you really should. But when you buy into these negative thoughts that others have about you, and develop a further sense of negative self-concept, you may end up feeling a lot of shame.

You learned a lot about shame in the last chapter and how severely it can affect people. Even in someone without a history of trauma, it can lead to behaviors like self-harm, including eating and substance abuse disorders, and suicidal ideation. The effect is even stronger when trauma is added into the mix.

Once the lens that you have to view yourself is tainted by negative self-concept, it's hard to see things clearly. Because you feel badly about yourself, all your interactions with other people seem negative, or that other people don't care about you. The smallest sign of neglect or omission helps support the bad image of yourself that you carry around.

Even if someone is genuinely trying to help you, when you believe that you're not worth much, you'll be suspicious. You'll want to know what they have to gain by doing so, since you don't believe that anyone could want to help someone like you out of the goodness of their hearts. Your past and your trauma taught you that other people simply can't be trusted, and you've learned that lesson very well.

You'll find some techniques at the end of this chapter to help you stop the shame spiral and develop a more positive image of yourself. Remember that the negative image is the one that's false, because it's the one that developed from the trauma you survived. It's the better self-concept that is the true one.

CONSEQUENCES OF NEGATIVE SELF-CONCEPT

We all know what confident people look like. They don't mind (or at least appear not to mind) entering a room full of strangers and introducing themselves. They're the ones volunteering for new projects at work and walking around with their spines straight and their shoulders back. Confidence brings optimism and trust with it, and these types of people have a positive self-concept of themselves.

On the flip side, there are a variety of ways in which someone with a negative view of themselves acts and thinks. They also hold true for people who don't see themselves accurately (which is true for most people with a negative self-concept) and for those who don't really understand who they are.

Fear of rejection/abandonment

All human beings have the fear of rejection or abandonment to some degree. Recall that our *Homo sapiens* ancestors survived by joining together in small groups. Being shunned by the others in the village or being abandoned by the tribe might very well have meant certain death in those days. One person doesn't have much of a chance against a hungry predator.

For trauma survivors, rejection confirms the belief that they already have of themselves as being unworthy and/or unlovable, or that they're really all alone on the planet. It's associated with psychological pain and suffering, of which most C-PTSD sufferers already experience enough of without adding on rejection.

There are plenty of ways that someone with this fear can try to avoid it, whether knowingly or not. They can abandon other people first, before the other has a chance to hurt them. Or they can draw back and create distance from others. Or hold back their true thoughts and feelings.

For example, a trauma survivor might pick a fight with their best friend which leads to a rift in the relationship. That avoids the risk that they'll be abandoned. Or they never talk about their pain with friends, who then wonder why someone who's so "together" is so distant and cold.

Reluctance to take risks

When it comes to uncertain outcomes (which is really what risk is about), the untraumatized human brain has two contradictory systems that sometimes conflict. On the one hand, the brain is wired for preferring novelty. New things are exciting, and you get a reward of pleasure neurochemicals when you experience them. It helped motivate humans as a species to explore their world and learn.

On the other hand, your brain wants to keep you alive. Going into the underbrush where you can't see what's happening could result in being eaten by a tiger, so there is a part of the brain that's risk-averse too.

Consider the people you know or have heard about who enjoy doing things like bungee-jumping, free climbing mountains (without safety ropes), or surfing huge waves. Or who don't mind getting in (and then out of) steamy love affairs, or who always want to take on the latest difficult project at work.

You can probably guess that their novelty system is much more active. They're happy to take on these risks that might seem way too big for other people, so clearly the risk aversion centers aren't taking over.

What else might you think about them? Do they seem timid or shy? What kind of self-concept do you think they operate under? Even if you don't know them personally, you can probably spot their confidence in themselves. They're willing to take on these risks because they're sure they can pull it off. They have a very positive self-concept.

On the other side of the coin are all the people whose risk adversity is much stronger than the pleasure they receive from trying new things. Some of this might be due to the fact that they don't realize it doesn't actually take that much novelty. You don't have to go bungee jumping in the Grand Canyon but can take a new route to work or to the store.

Those with C-PTSD aren't convinced they can take risks and come out unscathed. They've been scarred by the trauma, and having a negative self-concept prevents people from being able to get past that fear of risk. They don't think of themselves as being successful or having the capacity to conquer challenges. It's much safer to avoid as much risk as they can.

Extreme self-protection

When it comes to interpersonal relationships, there's a spectrum of the ways that people can act. At one end of the spectrum is self-exposure, where the person allows themselves to be fully vulnerable to the other. They let down their guard and permit the other person to get to know who they truly are.

The other end is self-protection, where the person doesn't trust the other one fully enough to let them in or expose weakness. For many trauma survivors, exposing weaknesses leads to more trauma, so they usually come down much closer to this end of the range.

Someone who's trying to protect themselves, in addition to not trusting other people, is always looking for potential threats coming from others. It's similar to hypervigilance but takes place in the relationship arena.

If your fear is that your romantic partner will leave you, you're constantly looking for signs that you're right. Are they wearing a different perfume or cologne than they were yesterday? Why did it take them an extra fifteen minutes to get home at rush hour? Why did they suddenly decide to wear a tie or scarf they haven't worn for months—are they meeting someone?

Or you may try to distance yourself from another person, even a friend. You're concerned that they're going to hurt you, and so you back away. You might believe on some level that creating some distance between you will lessen the inevitable pain when they leave or abandon you.

Once you're convinced that the person is ready to bail on you, you might start treating them rudely or knock them down a peg. You're thinking that it'll hurt much less when they eventually do take off, because they weren't that great to begin with and really, they've done you a favor by removing themselves from your life.

There are times when people do need to protect themselves in a relationship. The other person might be an energy vampire, taking up too much time and thought. Or they might be abusive, or they may be trying to work a scam. It's wise not to get close to these types of people once their true nature is revealed.

However, for many C-PTSD sufferers, they protect themselves against every single person they know and meet. There's no chance for them to find the kind of intimacy that will help them recover, because they can't allow themselves to be even a little bit vulnerable.

Difficulty with relationships whether romantic or platonic

Extreme self-protection is one obstacle that gets in the way of nurturing relationships. And when you're convinced that you're worthless or weak, you don't understand why anyone would want to be your friend or partner. Your lack of trust gets in the way.

Another issue is that you may (again, unintentionally) seek out relationships that will be destructive or harmful. People without a disorder who tend to be positive in their outlook find it very hard to spend time with someone who's constantly down on themselves. The positive types want to "fix" their friends, and then get frustrated when nothing changes.

Traumas are difficult for people who haven't gone through them to wrap their heads around. Because your positive friends have probably always been that way, they really don't understand how someone could genuinely feel that badly about themselves.

They often give advice, such as to get more exercise or more sunshine or think about the things you're grateful for. These tips often do work for someone without a disorder who's temporarily feeling blue or sad. But they're ineffective for someone who's experienced complex trauma.

After trying and failing to get you to think better about yourself, the way that they feel about you, they might give up or at least spend less time with you. You've probably heard it said that misery loves company, so another person who thinks badly about themselves is more likely to hang out with you. Or someone who is attracted to people with negative self-concept because they're bullies or otherwise have their own issues about healthy relationships.

Either way, negative self-concept is a recipe for unhealthy relationships.

Unconstructive thinking patterns that reinforce the negative self-image

You've already learned about the way that neural pathways that get used become stronger, while those that aren't are weakened and pruned back. This happens whether the pathway leads to constructive or unconstructive results.

The more you think negative thoughts, the stronger they become and the harder it is to think positively. It's a vicious cycle.

For example, you feel like you're alone and isolated because of the trauma that you've been through. You meet someone for a date at a local restaurant, and you're nervous about what they might think of you. They turn their head to catch the waitress's eye while you're talking, which you see as a sign of rejection.

Now, everything they do is under scrutiny. Did they look at the cute person at the next table for just a little too long? Did they drop their spoon on the floor because they were careless, or didn't want to look at you anymore?

You might start drinking to take the edge off, but in any case, it's clear to you that they don't like you and there's no chance of a second date. So, you pick a fight or start arguing with them over nothing to cut them down to size, and that's the end of the date.

You can't sleep that night thinking about how they didn't like you or think you were worthy. What you saw on the date only reinforced your view that you're unlovable. And so, the cycle continues, as you continue to search for clues that you're right about yourself and wind up confirming your beliefs.

Less able to solve problems

Thinking is hard for the human brain. It requires the use of a resource that we haven't really had for all that long, compared to how long the lizard brain structures have been on the planet. It's slow work. The brain would really rather conserve energy and go back to using the lizard brain and rules of thumb instead of all this tiring reasoning and problem solving.

If there's no way that the brain can solve a problem using this slow, inefficient system, then why should it waste its time with that resource? If you look at the problem and can't even see how you could start to solve it, what's the point? You give up before you start. There's no point in doing all that work when you're not going to resolve anything.

This is especially true for trauma survivors who don't think very much of themselves. They don't think they're smart enough to solve puzzles that seem a little more complex, so they won't try to in the first place.

The other factor is that with all the hyperarousal and activity that's going on in the brain, there's less capacity for the brain to switch over to logical thinking and problem solving. It's already using up a lot of fuel keeping you alert to danger.

When you're under threat, the brain doesn't think you have time for all the slow processing of facts that problem solving requires. It wants you to survive, and logic can come later after the tiger's gone. Of course, for C-PTSD sufferers, the tiger is never gone so there's never a good opportunity for using reasoning skills.

Can't address their own wants and needs

Have you ever thought about what an earthworm wants when you see it on the sidewalk? Whether it likes the sun, or wants some food, or maybe the company of another earthworm? You've probably never given much thought to what an earthworm needs, because it's not really worthy of your consideration. It's too low down on the food chain for you to think about.

Unfortunately, many complex trauma survivors feel they're roughly on the same level when it comes to value or worth as an earthworm. Why should they think about their own wants and needs, much less express them to someone else? Who cares about worms?

They may not even be able to admit to themselves what their wants and needs are. For example, someone who's feeling alone and alienated doesn't want to think about their desire for intimacy with another person. That will probably make them sadder and more depressed, and even more isolated than they already are.

They're certainly not going to express these needs to another person, because they've learned that other humans are not trustworthy. Talking about what they want might just be an open invitation to be rejected or abandoned by others, so it's much safer to ignore them.

Did any of these effects resonate with you? Do you feel like you're in a downward spiral and that everything you do and everyone you talk to is just reinforcing the negative image you have of yourself? Remember that a wholly negative image is a false one. You may feel like you're a worm, but you're not. Maybe you'll never actually be your ideal self, but you can get much closer to it and feel that you're much closer to it than you do right now.

COGNITIVE DISTORTIONS

It's very common for survivors of complex trauma to think in ways that don't always line up with reality. Thinking that someone doesn't like you because they turned their head away briefly while you were speaking is a cognitive distortion. What you're thinking is inconsistent with what's actually happening in reality.

You might think to yourself that as a result of your trauma that you'll always be afraid. Whenever that thought appears, you'll likely experience a mix of uncomfortable emotions, such as shame, helplessness, frustration, and sadness. The more this thought reoccurs (and as you know that neural pathway gets stronger and stronger the more it's used), the more you will be afraid.

Similarly, once you start thinking that you'll never be able to get over your depression, you'll start thinking more about feeling depressed and your inability to change it. You'll feel sad, hopeless, and down. The more you feel this way, the more likely you are to begin (or continue) isolating yourself from others. You'll start finding excuses to avoid the activities that previously brought you joy. Which, in turn, will make you feel more depressed.

But when you step back from these thoughts, you can see that they're cognitive distortions, or maladaptive thoughts. Because you probably haven't always been depressed in the past, and experienced times when the depression lifted, even if you're prone to it.

Likewise, it's not realistic to think that you will always be depressed for the rest of your life. Even if it's not treated, depression has a tendency to come and go. You learned earlier in the book about recency bias, which is a systemic thinking error where what's happened most recently seems the most important. That can affect your thoughts as well.

There are a number of these distortions that are common to humanity, whether or not someone is suffering from C-PTSD. As with many of the symptoms and effects you've already learned about, most people without the disorder will occasionally have these thoughts themselves. But for them it's usually fleeting, or something they can shake off relatively easily. But if you have C-PTSD, these thoughts can greatly affect your actions, and you can't let go of them quickly or easily.

Catastrophizing

When you immediately assume the worst outcome for yourself, particularly if something goes wrong, you're catastrophizing. Even if it's not the most likely outcome, it's the one that you're drawn to, ignoring others that are more realistic.

For example, suppose someone you know without an anxiety disorder lost their job. If you're friends with them, you would probably assure them that they would soon get another job. They might simply need to rework their resume, start networking, or take some other actions now that they're unemployed.

After the shock of losing their job is over—and I've certainly lost jobs before myself, so I know how much of a shock it can be! —the friend will get into action to find another position. It might take some time, but they'll work on it. This is commonly what happens when people lose their jobs; eventually they'll find work.

For someone who catastrophizes, though, the mind automatically goes to the worst-case scenario of never finding another position again, for the rest of their lives. They might go even further and decide that the job loss means that they'll lose their home and family and eventually end up in a homeless encampment.

These terrible outcomes are certainly possible, but they're not likely. The problem with dwelling on them is two-fold. One, all the rumination continues to make the neural pathways stronger, so traveling down the road to catastrophe in your mind becomes easier and easier.

The second is that if you believe this is your likely destination, then you won't take the actions that lead to better results. You don't ask someone to help you improve your resume. You don't search job boards on the Internet to find who's hiring people like you. And you ignore the networking opportunities in your area. Avoiding all these things makes the adverse events more likely, which is the exact opposite of what you want.

All or none (black or white)

In reality, life is made of nuances and shades of gray. Though taking too many drugs is considered bad, not everyone who does so is a bad person. Getting top grades is common for smart people, but occasionally doing badly doesn't make you dumb. In many situations, there are more than two possible results.

However, those with C-PTSD often take an all-or-nothing approach when it comes to life, especially for themselves. Either you're bad, or you're good. Either you're smart, or you're dumb. Either you're weak, or you're strong. If you get a raise or get promoted at your job, you're successful, if you don't, you're a failure.

Another aspect of life on this planet is that humans make mistakes. All of us get things wrong, say the wrong thing, don't understand the context of the situation which leads to an error, and so on. No matter whether you're good or bad, smart or dumb, weak or strong, no one gets it right all the time.

Therefore, in reality no one is all good or all bad, totally smart or completely dumb, utterly weak or strong. There are times when good people do bad things or make bad decisions. This holds true for everyone, whether they have a disorder or not.

When you start thinking that any bad move (like taking drugs) turns you into a bad person, or that weakness on your part when it comes to something like intimacy makes you a weak person, you're strengthening the deconstructive pathways. And just like with catastrophizing, you begin acting in a way that runs counter to what you really want.

Once you perceive that you've become a bad person, you might feel guilty and ashamed and prevent yourself from doing things you like because you don't think you deserve them. Or you might increase the "bad" behavior, because in for a penny, in for a pound.

Minimizing the positive, or "filtering"

When you feel badly about yourself it's hard to see anything in a positive light. Whatever's happened to you previously that was good you decide was due to luck or chance, being in the right place at the right time or knowing the right people.

You might believe that you got the job you love because you knew someone at the company, not because you have a degree or solid experience in the subject and did your best to wow them at the interview.

Or you went out to lunch with a friend of yours and they mentioned that they don't like your new hairstyle. You found the rest of the discussion pleasant and fun and enjoyed yourself, but once you get home all you can think about is that comment about your hair. You fixate on the one unpleasant detail until it's almost all you remember of your lunch. Now you're angry or upset at your friend and thinking about what a horrible meal you had with them.

Which isn't what really happened that day. But as happens with this type of cognitive distortion, you magnified the small, negative detail until it cast a shadow over the entire experience.

Labeling

Everyone labels themselves and other people. It's a shortcut for our minds that helps conserve energy, and we rely on rules of thumb to get us through the day. Everyone who drives a certain type of car is a jerk. People who go to Ivy League schools are smart. People who go to Ivy League schools are rich. Anyone who wears unusual jewelry is interesting.

The issue is that people with C-PTSD are overly rigid in their labels and don't allow for the kind of nuance that exists in reality. You're probably particularly rigid when it comes to labeling yourself, thinking things like "I'm a loser" or "I'm weak". As you can probably see, this goes hand-in-hand with all-or-nothing thinking.

Taking things personally

Of course, from time to time most people take a comment that wasn't aimed at them as a personal attack or statement about them. Yet for many with C-PTSD, nearly everything that goes wrong or is a negative issue is directly related to something they've done, or because there is something wrong with them.

For example, you may text a friend of yours and not hear back immediately, which is unusual for them. If you take this personally, you might rack your brains to figure out what you said to anger or upset them. You'll reread your message several times to see what you said that was offensive. If you try hard enough, you can probably come up with something.

After you've worked yourself up into believing that you did something wrong, and potentially catastrophizing it into feeling that this friend has dumped you and will never talk to you again, you get a text from them saying that they were in a meeting where phones had to be silenced. Or they were driving somewhere and couldn't respond.

The reality is that other people's behavior is usually more about them than about you. Just as you're mostly concerned with yourself and you're the most important person in your life, other people are mostly thinking about themselves, not you or anyone else. Believing that you're the reason other people do what they do is not a true reflection of what's going on.

Misunderstanding control

Just as you don't have control over anyone else's actions, they don't have control over yours. But a common cognitive distortion is believing that control is located anywhere else besides the person themselves. There are two related fallacies when it comes to control.

One is the fallacy of external control, where everything that happens to you is the result of someone or something else and there's nothing you can do to change it. You didn't get promoted because your boss, or others in the organization, don't like you or preferred the other guy who did get the promotion. Whatever occurs in your life is fate and you're completely helpless to make any changes.

When you don't take responsibility for your own actions, you can't grow as a person and you can't get what you want. It may be true that your boss likes your colleague more than you, but that could also be due to the fact that you often show up late to work and you take more time to get everything done.

While there certainly are things that happen in life that are beyond anyone's control, like accidents or natural disasters, the fact is that the only one who has control over your actions is you. Whether or not your boss likes you doesn't affect whether you get up in time to make it to work (at least not directly), and it doesn't affect whether you get your work done in a timely fashion or if you take too long playing around on social media.

The internal control fallacy is where you believe that your actions directly affect other people's emotions, thoughts, and actions. Because you said something negative, you made the other unhappy. Or you did something that caused another person to feel badly about themselves.

Believing that you affect other people's lives to such an extent is the flip side to taking everything personally. Your friend may be unhappy because their spouse lost a job, or their grandfather died, or they read an article that made them feel sad. None of these things has to do with anything that you said or did.

Reading others' minds

Similarly, it's not realistic to believe that you know what's going on in anyone else's head. Even if you believe that their actions or words are a clue, you still might be getting it wrong.

For example, you might conclude that your counselor thinks you're a waste of time. This might be based on nothing more than your own distorted view of yourself. Or maybe during a session the counselor fidgeted in their chair or looked out the window as you were talking.

But you have no way of knowing that the reason they fidgeted or glanced away is because they think you're a waste of time. They might be fidgeting because they've been sitting in the desk chair for too long.

Maybe their leg started itching and fidgeting was a good way to scratch it. They looked out the window because seeing the landscape helps them think about what you were saying. In other words, there are a lot of reasons why people do things, and many of them are not related to you.

Or it is related to you, but they haven't reached the conclusion that you believe they have. The counselor fidgeted because it's something you've said to them many times, but you haven't taken the action they recommended. That doesn't mean that they think you're a waste of time; they just think you'd be in a better place if you took their suggestion.

Changing others

If only you pushed hard enough or persuaded with the right words, the other person would do exactly what you want and then you'd both be happy. Part of the distortion here is believing that once someone else makes the right changes that would fix everything. The other part is believing that you can change another person.

You might not be happy to get what you think you want, either because that's not what you really want or what you want won't make you happy. Maybe you think that you can be happy once your partner wears the right clothes. But even if you get them to dress differently, they might still not be right for you.

"Shoulding"

It's common to think there is a right way for everyone to act, and they "should" act that way. Including you. So, when you don't do the things you "must" do, such as attain a certain body weight or shape, you'll be upset with yourself. And if someone else "breaks" a rule by acting differently, you'll probably be upset and angry with them.

The reality is not everyone on the planet behaves with the same iron-clad rules and expecting them to only leads to anger and frustration on your part. And if you're using "should" to help motivate yourself towards some kind of ideal behavior, you're setting yourself up to feel guilty and ashamed when you don't do those things you "ought" to do.

Reasoning emotionally

If something feels a certain way, then you might erroneously believe it to be true. For example, you feel like you're a weak person because you weren't able to escape or evade the trauma that happened to you. Since you feel weak, then you believe it must be true that you are weak.

Emotions can be very strong and overrule logical thinking. In fact, logically if you were able to survive the trauma, then you must be strong enough to have done so. Which means you're not truly weak, even though you feel like you are.

Overgeneralizing

With this distortion, people believe that the world is a certain way based on one piece of evidence, or one event. So, if you receive one bad review at work, you may believe that you're really bad at your job, or incompetent in some way.

The issue here is that the situation can become self-fulfilling if you dwell on it for too long or take action (or fail to take action) based on the one event. If you believe that you're bad at your job, then you won't take the steps that your supervisor recommended to improve. You won't take the class you need, or work with your boss to develop an action plan. If you think you're incompetent, you won't take risks that you need to show how competent you really are.

"Heaven's reward"

If you believe that there's a force or energy keeping score, you might think that you'll eventually be rewarded for certain kinds of sacrifices, or by denying yourself certain things. When you make the sacrifices or act in self-denial and then don't get the reward you expected, you might become angry or resentful.

The truth is that life isn't fair. You won't always get what you want, and if you measure every situation in terms of its "fairness" you may end up feeling hopeless when things don't work out the way you believe they "should."

Cognitive distortions and negative self-concept can affect C-PTSD sufferers not only by making you feel badly about yourself, but also interfering with how you interact with others. It gets in the way of your relationships with family and friends, and alters how you behave in public and around others. Fortunately, there are techniques you can use to help you improve your view of yourself.

BUILDING A MORE ACCURATE AND POSITIVE SELF-CONCEPT

The cognitive distortions and negative lens that you view yourself with both involve an error in engaging with reality. The truth is that the complex trauma has led to an inaccurate and destructive perception of yourself. Part of recovery is seeing these distortions for what they are and increasing your ability to see reality for what it is.

Thoughts and emotions are generated by the human brain, but what you think and feel doesn't define who you are. Having the capacity to distance yourself from these activities will help you choose what you want to take action on, instead of reacting as if everything you feel is actually true about the world. Though it's crucial for those with C-PTSD to be able to do this, it's important to anyone's mental health to be able to recognize when to let certain thoughts and emotions go without reacting to them automatically.

Many activities can help you learn to detach from your thoughts, and one that's common is meditation. It'll help you learn to let feelings and thoughts go. There are plenty of ways to meditate, but a good way to start is with a guided meditation. You'll be listening to someone guide you through pleasant imagery or things to focus on, and it's often a lot easier for beginners because having someone else talk helps keep your mind from racing all over the place.

You can find meditations online or by subscribing to an app. If you find a voice that's irritating for whatever reason, try another one. You'll find a lot to choose from, so don't give up if your first try is more annoying than relaxing or you don't like their style of meditation.

Later in this book you'll find some specific exercises that will help you see yourself more accurately. It's critical for you to be able to look at your thoughts objectively, so that you can determine which ones you should pay attention to and which ones should be let go. You are not your thoughts and not your emotions either.

Notice self-critical thoughts

As you go through your day, try to pause whenever you recognize that you're having a negative thought about yourself. For example, if you think "I'm so clumsy" when you drop something, or "I'm so dumb" when someone points out something you think should have been obvious, or "I'm crazy" or whatever thoughts cross your mind that aren't positive about yourself.

Just noticing the thoughts, without judgement, often surprises people when they do this because they have no idea how many times a day they're talking or thinking badly about themselves. Don't feel bad about yourself for feeling bad about yourself either—it's very common!

Acknowledging that you're not speaking well of yourself helps you see that your mental commentary is likely not doing you any favors. In fact, you might conclude that it's no surprise how down on yourself you are, given how often the unconstructive thoughts come up.

Determine how true they are

Look at these thoughts objectively. Everyone drops things from time to time, even those who are trained to catch and hold onto objects. Ask any major league baseball player how often the ball slides right through their mitt!

Likewise, everyone misses what's right in front of their noses some-times. (Ask any mother whose child can't find what they want in the fridge.) Does missing the obvious really make you dumb? If so, pretty much everyone on the planet is dumb as well.

Think about what evidence you have to support the negative statement you made, as well as what evidence you have against it. Suppose you told yourself that you're dumb because you sent out a document that had grammar mistakes in it. Is that evidence that you're dumb? Or is it evidence that you made errors? Your boss has told you that they rely on your intelligence to get things done, and you can look back on smart choices you've made in the past: evidence against.

We all make mistakes, we all miss what's in front of us, and most of us have done dumb or bad things at least once in our lives. I don't recommend that people go out and get drunk but doing so doesn't make you a bad person. Just because you do something that might not have been such a hot idea, it doesn't mean that you should label yourself negatively over it.

Speak positively to yourself

Many people talk differently to themselves than they would to a friend or loved one. For example, when your friend loses a job, you'll reassure them that any other company would be lucky to have them. Why don't you tell yourself the same thing if it happens to you? Be as kind to yourself as you would be to someone else you love in a similar situation.

When you catch your negative thought, you can try to reframe it right away. For example, if you catch yourself saying "I'm a loser" because you made an error at work, remind yourself that everyone makes mistakes and not being perfect makes you human, not a loser.

Feel embarrassed about dropping something? Tell yourself (or anyone who's listening) that you meant to put that right there.

Write down your good qualities and positive things that you know to be true about yourself. Pull the list out periodically and remind yourself that you do have plenty going for you. You don't have to look at the list only when you're feeling bad. Just give yourself a little boost in the middle of the day. These positive neural pathways will grow stronger as you do.

Reduce shame-bearing opportunities

If there are particular situations that tend to trigger feelings of shame, avoid them if you can. If not, prepare in advance and think about how you can reduce the chances you'll feel ashamed.

For example, suppose you know that your boss is going to call you in because you did something wrong. How could you avoid or lessen the shame you might feel? Maybe by determining how it went wrong and deciding to show the boss that you learned from the mistake. That will demonstrate that you take accountability and also that you understand how to avoid it in the future... all of which is what your boss wants to hear anyway.

Learn to reduce judgments

Holding people, including yourself, up to impossibly high standards is a recipe for failure and shame. If you judge yourself a lot, you probably judge other people as well. And that's a recipe for not having a lot of relationships.

A lot of judgment comes from a place of believing that people know better, and "should" do better, but they're just not doing it. What if you assumed that everyone was doing the best they could at any given moment, including yourself?

None of us can always be at our best, and sometimes you might be running into someone who's not at their best, for reasons that have nothing to do with you. The kind way to act is to assume that they just were overwhelmed. Or that they have different standards and they're meeting their own, which don't happen to be yours.

Ignore the "shoulds"

Thinking that you "should", "ought", or "must" do something is another recipe for failure. It sets you up to feel badly about yourself when you inevitably fall short. Think about why you're not doing something that you feel you should do, or why you're doing something people say you shouldn't.

For example, take the perennial New Year's resolution of "I should lose weight." With that attitude, you won't lose it! Think about why you want to lose weight—maybe you have health issues, maybe you want to look good at a reunion, maybe you just hate buying large-sized clothes because they're not as nice as the smaller sizes.

Now, why haven't you lost the weight? And no judgment! It's not because you're lazy or doomed to be overweight for the rest of your life. Maybe you grew up eating a certain way that was heavy on the processed foods and fat and light on veggies and fruit, and now it's a problem that you're older. Maybe you weigh too much because you've always leaned on food for comfort, and you're extra stressed out at the moment.

Or you always ate a bit more than you really needed, but you exercised it off every day at the gym. Now ask yourself, why aren't you exercising every day at the gym? Maybe you don't have time between getting the kids off to school and yourself to work. Maybe you actually hated working out but did it anyway, and now you have no patience to do things that you dislike. Or you used to go in the mornings before work, which you no longer can because your schedule changed, and the gym isn't open early enough for you to make it to work on time anymore.

Instead of shoulding yourself into making temporary changes that go away as soon as life gets busy or stressful again, think about the choices you can make. You can choose to lose weight to buy cute clothes again, and you'll choose to find a way of eating healthier in order to do so.

Live your own life

A woman who had worked for years with people who were dying asked her patients what their biggest regrets were. And the number one regret that they had was that they hadn't lived a life that was true to themselves.

Everyone has their own ideas about what's worth doing, what they love to do and how they want to spend their time. The people who love you want you to do well in life, but they may have specific ideas as to how you should go about it. Parents and grandparents have ideas that are rooted in the time and culture that they grew up in, which may no longer be true today.

For example, up until very recently many working Americans had one job at a company that they worked at for years and which provided them a pension in retirement. Someone from that background might think it best that you do the same thing, not realizing that the number of companies with pension plans is vanishingly small, and that it's now common and expected to move from job to job.

Your friends may have ideas for you too, as might your colleagues, supervisors, or others. But they're not you, and you're the only one who gets to live your own life. Do what you want to do, even if it's not popular or people think it's unusual (as long as it's legal!)

Change the impact of mistakes

With very few exceptions, modern educational and professional culture is not happy when people make mistakes. Even though errors are inevitable, given that no human is perfect, they're generally looked on as a bad thing and something that should be avoided whenever possible.

However, Silicon Valley and a few other companies have figured out that in order to keep up with the speed of modern technology, they need to try things and have them fail, then figure out what went wrong and improve it for the next round. "Fail fast and iterate" is the motto.

In other words, not only is failure not something to be avoided, it's to be embraced as quickly as possible so that the lessons can be learned, and the next iteration is better. What if you took on Silicon Valley's way of using a mistake, not as a cudgel to beat yourself with, but instead an opportunity to learn? And then take that lesson with you?

LACK OF MEANING

According to DESNOS, in addition to these alterations of thought and self-perception, there are also changes in the system of meaning. This is the difficulty in holding onto a system of faith, or even a belief that justice will eventually be served. Complex trauma can change your outlook on the whole world, including the way that it works or was designed. You might no longer believe that your life has a purpose, or that any life has a purpose

Some with C-PTSD might not believe that there's any real kindness or goodness in the world, that everything is based on selfishness. Or they might lose the hope that they'll ever be forgiven. Some may believe that there's nothing good that can happen to them in this world, because they only exist here to be hurt.

This despair and hopelessness tends to fluctuate over time, so there may be seasons where everything doesn't seem quite so hopeless, mixed in with times of complete despair. Survivors may come to accept what happened to them on a certain level, but have these issues bubble up again when they're ready to go deeper.

Another symptom is questioning the faith or ethics system in which they were raised. This sometimes leads to a belief that the spiritual head is in fact an agent of dark or malevolent forces instead.

Unfortunately, this can lead to a significant inability to make any changes. A complex trauma survivor who no longer believes that life or the world makes any kind of sense ends up in a persistent state of *learned helplessness*. It's what happens when you feel that you're unable to ever escape, and so you stop trying to change your circumstances.

Recovery from the disorder does require you to make some changes in order to help rewire your brain. If you're in a state of learned helplessness, you feel incapable of making choices, acting to support yourself, and making any adjustments that will help you feel better. However, you're not your thoughts and feelings. Just because at the moment you feel unable to do these things doesn't mean that you are actually unable to do them.

CHAPTER SUMMARY

Having a negative self-concept is having a negative view of yourself, one that doesn't match up with reality. Complex trauma brings cognitive distortions, where you think things that aren't necessarily true and lead to a more negative view of yourself and others. However, there are ways that you can learn to improve your relationship with reality and start thinking more constructively.

- Self-concept includes the way you view yourself, your evaluation of your own worth, and your ideal self.
- Having a negative self-concept leads to consequences such as fear of rejection, extreme self-protection, and an inability to understand and take care of your wants and needs.

- Negative self-concept also results in cognitive distortions such as all-or-nothing thinking, catastrophizing, difficulty with relationships, and believing you can read others' minds (usually to your detriment).

- You can build a more positive self-concept by methods such as ignoring "should" statements, noticing your self-critical thoughts and determining whether or not they're true, and reframing mistakes as opportunities to learn.

- The DESNOS criteria also includes a change in the systems of meaning, such that C-PTSD sufferers may no longer see a purpose in life or feel a sense of overwhelming despair and hopelessness.

In the next chapter you will learn about the third factor in a C-PTSD diagnosis which deals with interpersonal issues.

6

DISTURBED INTERPERSONAL RELATIONSHIPS

At this point in the book, you understand how important it was for the survival of humans to have relationships with other humans. Living together helped ward off predators, and by working together groups of people could kill large prey to feed the village or tribe. As a species, we are wired to be sensitive to other people and to enjoy bonding with them.

So much so that the human brain rewards us when we help or give to another person. There are three main neurochemicals that lead to a feeling of happiness, or the "Happiness Trifecta": dopamine, oxytocin, and serotonin (Ritvo, 2014).[1] In addition to the happiness part of the equation, each chemical is responsible for some other activities. You've probably heard of serotonin before, especially if you struggle with depression, because many of the medications that treat the condition work through increasing the availability of serotonin in the brain.

Dopamine is also important in motivation, and you may have heard of oxytocin as the cuddle hormone. When it's released, blood pressure decreases, as does the level of social fear. Trust, empathy, and bonding are all increased when oxytocin is flowing. Giving to other people activates the entire Happiness Trifecta. In other words, relationships are so important to us that our brain releases these three chemicals to encourage us to be happy by bonding more with each other.

That's why disturbed interpersonal relationships are such an issue for anyone who encounters these difficulties. You're missing out on happiness chemicals, and it's distressing for your brain which knows you need to bond with others to survive.

MASLOW'S HIERARCHY OF NEEDS

You may have heard of this concept before, as it's foundational to how science views the personal growth that a person can attain. It helps explain further why being successful in life requires healthy relationships.

Psychologist Abraham Maslow suggested that people are motivated by the need to achieve certain things, and that some needs are more pressing than others (Mcleod, 2020).[2] Imagine the various needs as levels in a pyramid. At the bottom is the largest tier, or the foundation of the most basic survival needs, and at the top is fully achieving your potential as a human being. The original pyramid had five levels, and this has been expanded in some theories, but the basics are the same.

1. Physiological needs (survival)

These are the requirements for functioning as a human being: food, water, rest, shelter, clothing, warmth, and sex. If you're deficient in this level because you're not getting basic needs met, you can't even think about the rest of the growth pyramid.

For example, children who are malnourished don't spend a lot of time learning in school. Their brains can't function properly because they don't have the required fuel. The brain won't want to waste energy on logic and reasoning when other, more important organs need the food instead.

Similarly, if you're constantly seeking shelter from the environment because you don't have a steady place to go, your brain is far more concerned about finding a safe spot than it is about learning subtraction.

Once most of these are taken care of, and they are for most people in developed countries, you can move on to the next level of needs.

2. Safety and security

People like some order and predictability in their environment, which gives them a measure of control and helps them feel safe. Family and society (when both are healthy) can provide this kind of security.

For example, a child who grows up going to school regularly, has a packed lunch or is able to get it at the school cafeteria, and can go to the nurse when they're not feeling well and get something to feel better has order in their lives.

Likewise, an adult who goes off every day to work and comes home to have dinner with the family has a predictable life. They can go to the doctor if they need medical care, send their kids to school, and have the financial stability to buy what they need.

Social stability is another important factor in security. Living in a neighborhood where there's little crime helps people feel safe. And having a police force that catches criminals and a justice system are additional predictors of security.

Someone who's living in a country at war or who is a refugee doesn't experience much of this, and neither do victims of violence and abuse. Having an abuser in the household means that days are unpredictable, because what didn't set them off yesterday could very well set them off today. Living in a region of chaos means that you can't rely on the police or the justice system to capture and deter criminals, who are then free to come after you.

When you've been able to bring a semblance of order and control to your situation, you're then ready to move up to the interpersonal level.

3. Belongingness and love

It's what this chapter is about: the need for healthy relationships with other people. Once someone is fed and clothed and sheltered, and feels reasonably safe in their home, they now turn to the social aspect of life.

Recall that humans who were evicted or shunned from their community in the early days of the species faced death, so having a "tribe" of some sort is built into the human psyche. It doesn't really matter which group, either: any group will do as long as you feel some identification with the others and that you belong.

This is necessary for every person, even those who might consider themselves *introverts* regardless of previous trauma. Introverts need time by themselves to relax and recharge, yet they still require some social interaction and support. Though they may not need as many friends as an *extrovert*, who revels and is energized by spending time with other people.

The need for belongingness consists of a variety of components: friendship, love, affection given and received, intimacy, acceptance, and trust. For someone who is unable to trust others due to the trauma they survived, this level is hard to fulfill. Trust is the basis of bonds with other people, and that in itself is difficult. Not to mention the rest of it, like affection and intimacy.

For those not suffering from a disorder, trust is not hard to come by and they find it easy to accept and be accepted by others. Their default assumption is that others mean well unless they prove otherwise, and relationships aren't held back by suspicions about others.

Once someone has a satisfactory sense of belonging to a group and having relationships, they can move on to the next level.

4. Esteem

Maslow classified this level into two categories: one, the need for external reputation such as status and prestige, and the second of internal esteem from dignity, mastery and independence. For children and teens, the external desire for status and being respected is more important.

As they develop into adults, the internal motivations become stronger. It's less important to achieve a reputation in the field as it is to master it, or to become independent and to achieve your goals.

As you might imagine, C-PTSD sufferers struggle with these as well. People who are abused as children don't feel respected. They have no status since they're the lowest on the totem pole. Their parent might not want to lash out at their spouse, so they lash out at the kids instead where there's less potential blowback. There's no prestige in being hurt or left.

In adulthood, not having been able to reach better status as a child makes it harder to achieve at work. Or even at home. Being able to move up the corporate ladder depends on making key contacts and relationships in the office or in the industry, which are hampered by the lack of healthy interpersonal skills.

On the other hand, those who are able to fulfill themselves internally and externally can make plans to advance. They'll see what they need to obtain to achieve their goals, which may be more schooling or a helpful friendship with a colleague and make those things happen for themselves.

After someone has been able to attain some degree of mastery in their chosen field and have the independence and status that they like, they can then begin to work on the highest and last level in the pyramid.

5. Self-actualization (realization of potential)

In order to reach your full potential, you need to have a solid foundation of self-esteem and compassion. You need to believe not only that you can do what you set out to do, but also that you deserve to be the best version of yourself that there is.

At this point you can focus on your personal growth and fulfillment. You can search out "peak experiences," which are the things that fill you with awe and wonder and where you lose all sense of time in the joy of the experience.

A peak experience occurs when you have a balance between your skill and the expected challenge. It's all-absorbing, and a variety of brain activities occur to facilitate it, which I won't get into in too much detail.

The important thing about the neuroscience behind peak experiences is that you can't be in a hyper-aroused state of threat. You have to be performing at optimal levels, which means your brain can't be consistently scanning for threats.

For example, some people have peak experiences while skiing extremely difficult trails, or bungee-jumping or engaging in similar physical activities. Is there any way that someone who is in fight-or-flight mode would be able to jump off a high bridge attached to some cords? Or decide to get off the ski lift at the top and see the twisting, dangerous trail below?

It's not just dangerous physical activities that can be peak experiences. Some people have them at very large concerts or religious services, where they can be caught up in the joy of all the people surrounding them and the music pumping through their veins. Not great for someone who doesn't trust people, who now is surrounded by hundreds or even thousands of them.

It takes most people a while to reach this level, if they ever do. Not everyone is able to reach their full potential. However, someone with C-PTSD has some things to take care of on the lower levels so they fulfill some more basic needs before they move on to self-actualization.

These five hierarchy levels aren't necessarily rigid, but most of one level must be satisfied before you can be comfortable working on the next level up. Sometimes you might be working on a higher level, and then for whatever reason dip back down into a lower one. However, the basic principle, which is that you need to mostly fulfill one level before you can start work on the next, holds true no matter the situation.

HEALTHY RELATIONSHIPS

Even those without C-PTSD can have difficulties with unhealthy relationships. What does a healthy one look like? It's helpful to know where you're diverging from a healthy place, so that you're aware of the way that it impacts your life and choose to do something differently. There are plenty of examples of dysfunctional relationships, so here's what a healthy one looks like.

It's based on mutual trust, respect, and honesty. (You probably can already see why they're so difficult for a complex trauma survivor, who has understandable issues about trust.) In a healthy partnership, both parties believe that the other has their best interests at heart and doesn't want to hurt them. When you're open and vulnerable to another, you do run the risk of getting hurt, but you understand that's not what they're trying to do.

Both parties respect each other. Obviously, different people have different strengths and weaknesses, but healthy partners believe that they're equals. Neither looks down at the other or feels that they're superior—or inferior. They're two adult humans who have their own minds and bodies, and they respect that each has *autonomy*, or the ability to make choices about their own minds and bodies.

They're honest with each other. If one isn't feeling cherished or respected, they explain this to the other without being confrontational. They don't want conflicts raging out of control, or to allow resentments to grow without telling the other person what's going on. Nor do they want to pretend that everything's fine if it's not. Healthy partners don't sulk or throw temper tantrums or freeze the other person out when they have a problem. Instead, they discuss it to find out if anything went wrong and needs to be fixed.

With all the trust they have in each other, they can be open and honest and communicate well together. This leads to emotional intimacy as they care for each other. In addition, the partners feel safe with each other, because they know the other one isn't going to punish them for no reason. They can share their feelings without concern for being rejected or criticized.

As emotional intimacy builds, so too does the commitment to each other. They want to make the partnership a success, so they're more willing to make compromises that will help keep them together. They are accountable to each other and responsible for whatever household tasks they each end up choosing. In a good partnership, tasks are shared between them so that no one person is shouldering a burden all by themselves.

Maybe most importantly, in a healthy relationship both partners encourage each other to grow and be the best versions of themselves that they can. That means taking risks, which are much easier when you feel safe and cared for, that the other person has your back in case something goes wrong.

Obviously, this is good for romantic relationships, but it can apply to friendships too. Being able to talk to a friend about what's going on in your life and not be worried that they'll reject you or laugh at you is an important part of life. You can have mutual respect and trust for people that you're not especially close to as well. It's the ideal way to relate to friends and family.

You can also extend the idea of healthy relationships to people that you work with. You may not be as close, and you might restrict the trust you have in them to whatever goes on in the office. Respecting your coworkers and supervisors and trusting them is key to having a robust relationship. They might be able to help you in your career, and vice versa. Similarly, you have an equal responsibility for the tasks in your group or department, and everyone communicates well and honestly with each other.

In real life, even people who don't have a disorder don't always have healthy relationships with everyone they know. They might have a dysfunctional family or family member, or colleagues with low levels of emotional intelligence. However, knowing what a healthy relationship looks like gives you something to look forward to. It may also help you determine whether a particular person will be healthy for you, which is important since many C-PTSD sufferers end up with the wrong partners.

WHY HEALTHY INTERPERSONAL RELATIONSHIPS ARE TOUGH ON COMPLEX PTSD PATIENTS

The nature of complex trauma, in addition to the brain's response to it, makes it very hard to form solid bonds with others. The brain is stuck in survival mode, always searching for threats. Which makes every single person you come across a potential danger, and certainly someone you can't trust.

No one can perceive someone as a threat to their very survival and simultaneously trust them with intimate truths about themselves. The protection instinct doesn't diminish, and so your brain is always trying to figure out what the other person's angle is and what they really intend to do. There's no chance for the other person to demonstrate their trustworthiness, and you won't be able to trust them.

Or you may be able to trust them a little bit and have some kind of relationship with them. But as soon as you perceive that they've messed up or abused your trust, you lose even that tiny bit of trust. Unfortunately, since everyone's human, it's likely they'll unintentionally do something to break that trust. A hyper-aroused brain will assume it was done with malicious intent, even though it may have been a completely innocent error.

The very nature of complex trauma makes it likely that the survivor's trust in other people was repeatedly broken and abused. In addition to a brain constantly searching for threats, they have solid evidence that people cannot be trusted.

This might most obviously be the case for those who suffered domestic and/or childhood abuse. In either case someone who was supposed to protect them, either spouse or parent, betrayed that trust over and over again during the time of the abuse. However, refugees and those who grew up in war-torn nations or other areas of chaos have the same issue. Their governments may have betrayed them, or the police that were supposed to protect them, or people in other organizations who repeatedly violated their trust.

Having difficulty regulating emotions is another reason why relationships can be so difficult for someone with the disorder. Whether you tend to lash out in anger, or are constantly extremely worried, or can't seem to get out of your negative moods very easily, partners can find this very difficult to live with. Not knowing what the triggers are for an outburst often makes the partner feel that they have to tiptoe around you, which adds additional stress onto them as well.

In general, there are two developmental issues that are directly impacted by C-PTSD and create problems with having healthy relationships. One of them is self-regulation, which you've already read quite a bit about. The other is attachment, or how people learn to have interpersonal relationships.

People who are able to develop normal interpersonal attachments experienced enough nurturing from their caregivers in childhood that they know other people will stick around. They don't tend to have abandonment issues, because they themselves were not abandoned or neglected when they were young. Children typically blame themselves for things that go wrong (for example, if their parents are getting divorced), but as they grow, they're able to understand that not everything is about them, and therefore, not everything is their fault. They know other people have different thoughts and experiences and that's what causes the actions that they take.

While those who developed a healthy attachment style may occasionally run into people who are not trustworthy, they don't assume that everyone is dangerous until proven otherwise. They can be vulnerable with other people, because in their experience other humans are trustworthy. And if someone else is not trustworthy, they can often see this ahead of time because they can spot the red flags of someone who may be neglectful, abusive, or otherwise not someone to get involved with.

By contrast, someone who survived complex trauma has a very different template for interpersonal interactions. They learned early on that anyone who "loves" (or is supposed to love them, like a parent) will either leave or hurt them, or both.

Not a recipe for being able to trust or rely on others, and dovetails with hypervigilance. If you know someone is going to leave you or hurt you, because in your experience that's all that can happen, then you'll be looking for signs that the person is thinking about leaving or hurting.

When it comes to danger and human evolution, what we as a species learned as we developed that we were better off seeing threats that didn't exist, as opposed to not seeing threats that did exist. If early humans saw grass waving and thought that meant a predator was lying in wait, they'd be able to flee.

If there was something in the grass, then they escaped death. If there wasn't something in the grass, they experienced fight-or-flight prep that ultimately wasn't necessary. It didn't do long-term damage. Acting on a potential threat had no bad consequences: either you survived a predator or some extra stress hormones. (Recall it's only the continuous or too-often release of stress hormones that damages your body, not the one-off, occasional bursts.)

On the other hand, if the early human didn't take the grass waving seriously and there was a predator, they might not survive the encounter. If there was nothing there, they were fine. In other words, not acting in the face of potential danger had potentially deadly consequences. We're the descendants of the ones that survived by taking threats seriously.

In someone who's hyper-aroused, that often means that every little signal is the potential sign of someone who's about to hurt or leave you. Are they wearing a different cologne? Did they look away while you were talking? Did they suddenly start going to the gym? Did they turn down an invitation to lunch because they said they were too busy? Did they take a little too long responding to your work email labeled "urgent"? This is all waving grass to someone with the leave-or-hurt template.

Being able to have (or develop) a supportive relationship is one of the factors in successfully recovering from C-PTSD. Most people who do recover have at least one of these partnerships in their life (Franco, 2017).[3] If you don't currently have one, it's not the end of the world, but it may take you a little longer to heal. At the end of this chapter you'll learn some techniques that will help you navigate the disorder with another person so that they understand what's going on.

SYMPTOMS OF RELATIONSHIP DIFFICULTIES

As you might imagine, there are a number of responses to that earlier, unhealthy template that sufferers of C-PTSD can demonstrate when it comes to relating to other people.

- Find trust hard (as this was already mentioned before, it is not discussed again here)
- Find intimacy hard

You already know how hard it is to trust people, which also makes it difficult to build close bonds with them. Intimacy is the mutual openness, willingness to share and be vulnerable that two people have with each other. It can be sexual as well but doesn't have to be. You can have intimate friendships and be intimate with family members as well.

In fact, there are four kinds of intimacy, all of which can be problematic for a survivor of complex trauma (GoodTherapy, 2019).[4] All of them take some time to develop and don't necessarily happen right away.

1. Experiential

This type of intimacy occurs when people build or strengthen their relationship through leisure activities. For example, if you play in a recreational soccer league, you could share this with your teammates.

2. Emotional

When you feel close enough to another person to share yourself, even when it's not something you're proud of. Someone with body image issues might consider telling their sister about it, knowing that she won't be hurtful about it.

3. Intellectual

Two people can enjoy discussing ideas and opinions with each other, even when they disagree. There's no need to win or compete on whose idea is better; they just enjoy the discussion and learning how the other thinks about the topic.

4. Sexual

This one is the type that many people first think of when they hear the word "intimacy." Not only can people be intimate with each other without sex, they can be sexual with each other without being intimate.

For example, one-night stands are often not so much about the bond between the two partners, but more about the sexual act itself.

In order to allow themselves to be vulnerable, which is an important element of intimacy, people have to feel some measure of security first. Allowing others to see who they really are, both good and bad, is risky. It could lead to rejection, and only those who are comfortable with that possibility can be so open with other people.

Even individuals who don't have a disorder sometimes have a tough time with being vulnerable. But it's particularly problematic for anyone with C-PTSD. They grew up in a world that wasn't safe for them, or have spent years in an unsafe environment. They haven't developed the sense of security that makes vulnerability possible.

Yet everyone wants intimacy of some kind. Complex trauma survivors may seek out relationships and want to build that closeness but pull away as soon as they become uncomfortable. This is puzzling and disappointing to their partners, who don't understand why they're involved in a relationship where they're pulled in, then pushed away repeatedly.

Sexual intimacy is often very challenging for those with C-PTSD, especially those who suffered sexual abuse. There is a lot of shame wrapped up in the act, in addition to any physical damage that may have occurred.

Choose the wrong partner

Many survivors of complex trauma know unhealthy relationships far better than they know healthy ones. They often end up with another abusive partner when it comes to romantic relationships.

For one thing, the survivors find abuse familiar. It's the healthy partners that seem strange or odd, because they have different behavior patterns than someone with C-PTSD is used to. Bad partners (abusive, neglectful, etc.) often display warning signs early on that would drive away anyone with a healthy attachment style. Since trauma survivors haven't been able to develop properly, they don't recognize the red flags that would scare off others.

In addition, as noted above, everyone wants intimacy, even if they don't really know how to go about it because they've never seen it in their own lives. Someone with the disorder may be so desperate to be loved that they're easy prey for an abusive partner. They may not be able to attract a healthy person, so they take what's available.

Or the survivor might be constantly searching for a rescuer. While the specific circumstances of the complex trauma may be long gone, the desire for someone to help them escape may not be.

This could lead to attachment with someone who appears to be a rescuer but is in fact abusive. Alternatively, they might demand that a non-abusive partner be the savior, which is hard on their partner.

May be preoccupied with the personal cause of the trauma

Especially when the trauma is due to abuse or personal violence, the survivor often becomes obsessed with the perpetrator (Richter, 2018).[5] They often see this person as all-powerful or unstoppable. Their own survival depended on their relationship with their tormentor, so they may be unable to let thoughts of the perpetrator go.

Always thinking about someone else creates problems in relationships, particularly romantic ones. Your partner might be upset that you still think about another person, long after that relationship is over.

Create tough living situations for other people

C-PTSD sufferers don't intend to make life hard for their partners, but it usually winds up being the case due to the nature of the trauma. Given that triggers can be unpredictable, even for the survivors, their partners don't know what will set off a scene or emotional outburst, or even total withdrawal.

You learned in Maslow's hierarchy of needs that after the basic needs have been satisfied (food, shelter, clothing) the next level is for safety: predictability and order. Someone living with a trauma survivor loses that sense of predictability in their lives to some extent.

The one with the disorder feels guilty or ashamed when they have an outburst or are otherwise triggered, so they may want to isolate themselves from their partner. Unfortunately, that just makes their partner feel even more rejected.

Even something as simple as a disagreement can make for a truly tense situation if the survivor is triggered and unable to regulate themselves during the discussion. Their partner may be reluctant to bring up any disagreements because they don't want to set the C-PTSD sufferer off. At the same time, they're likely to feel resentment that they can't communicate the way they want.

That resentment can build over time until the partner feels they can no longer be a part of the survivor's life. This only reinforces that early template that people who love you will either hurt you or leave.

IMPROVING YOUR RELATIONSHIPS

While the issues covered above are significant, they're not insurmountable if you're willing to do some work. You'll also need a partner who understands what's going on and is willing to work with you as well. There is hope and you can learn to develop strong bonds with other people.

Have you ever heard the saying that sunlight is the best disinfectant? It comes from a former US Supreme Court justice, Louis Brandeis. He was talking about the benefit of publicity. Transparency, or bringing issues into the bright light of the sun, is the best method of avoiding corruption in public policy (and management). But it's also true for relationships, which require honesty.

One of the best things you can do for potential partners is to be honest about your C-PTSD and the ways that it demonstrates in your actions. There are a number of websites that you can point to (and many referenced in this book) to help your partner understand what it is and how it affects your daily life. There are things that people without the disorder take for granted, and they may not recognize that the reason you don't do the same thing is because of the disorder.

You'll probably still have to explain after a triggering situation what happened. They'll understand it as a function of the disorder, not how you feel about them, if you've previously been open about it. It's important that they know many of your actions aren't personally biased against them but are a reaction to what happened to you earlier in your life.

You can also discuss some of your likely triggers. If you can see a pattern for some of your actions, you can let them know what's likely to cause a reaction. Not only will they understand when it happens, but they can also help you avoid the situation.

For example, suppose one of your triggers is a dark alley. If you let your friends know, they'll try to avoid the bars that open off a dark alley and go into the brighter ones or those with entries on a bright sidewalk instead. Bear in mind that you may have to remind people more than once. This lets you practice not taking things personally and recognizing that other people have a variety of things on their minds.

Another great tactic is to see a therapist or counselor who specializes in C-PTSD. Even someone who loves you and wants you to heal and be well isn't equipped to handle everything that the disorder throws at you. Rather than overwhelming a loved one or friend by asking for help that they just aren't capable of, find someone who understands how to provide that kind of assistance.

A professional won't make you feel bad or guilty about the trauma and how it's impacted your life. They can help you look back to see if you can find any patterns in your triggers. You also may sometimes have unconstructive thoughts about your partner and a therapist is a much better person to discuss those with! They provide objective guidance, and you can be honest with them because you don't have to worry about hurting their feelings.

Therapists are there to help you, specifically. Unless you're in couples counseling (and you can certainly be in both), the counselor wants to help guide you to the best outcome for you, not necessarily the best outcome for your partner.

Anyone who's involved with you, either friends or family or sexually, has mixed motives because they need to take care of themselves as well. They bring their own biases and experiences to the table, which may result in them giving advice that's not helpful or even counter-productive. Not because they're out to get you, but simply because they don't know any better.

A counselor who's experienced with C-PTSD sufferers knows that you probably don't have the knowledge you need to determine who's a healthy partner for you or not. At least not yet. They can help you identify warning signs in potential partners, with no ulterior motive than assisting you in the healing process.

You might have noticed that both of these recommendations entail asking for help, which can be very difficult for complex trauma survivors. You have to trust that the people you're asking will provide it and not use your pain against you. It's also critical to recognize that asking for help does not make you weak.

In fact, asking for help shows strength because you are taking that risk. Though it may seem like a huge risk to you, remember that people love to help others. It's ingrained in the human brain to make us happy by releasing the trifecta of pleasure neurochemicals: serotonin, oxytocin, and dopamine. When you're asking for help, you're actually giving these other people a chance to feel a wash of happiness.

It's not really as one-sided as many people think it is. Yes, you're receiving help. But your helpers are getting something out of it too, even if they don't know it. As you get stronger, you'll also have the opportunity to help others and release the Happiness Trifecta in your own head.

CHAPTER SUMMARY

Difficulty with interpersonal relationships is one of the key markers for C-PTSD. It can make you and the people around you miserable until you start taking steps to counteract it. You can learn techniques to make building bonds with other people easier, which is important because we all need relationships to thrive as people.

- Maslow's hierarchy of needs shows that after satisfying basic necessities like food and shelter and being safe and secure, people are motivated to fulfill themselves through relationships.
- Healthy relationships are based on mutual trust and respect,

and are characterized by the support each gives the other in fulfilling their potential.

- Due to the nature of complex trauma and the way that it impacts survivors, relationships are hard for them to develop and sustain.

- Relationship problems include difficulties with intimacy, trust, choosing the wrong partner, being obsessed with their tormentor, and creating a chaotic environment.

- Explaining to others the nature of the disorder and how you typically express it, as well as finding an experienced therapist, are helpful for improving interpersonal relationships.

In the next chapter you will learn techniques to help you on your road to recovery.

7

RECOVERING AND RECLAIMING YOUR IDENTITY

Healing from complex trauma isn't easy. If it was, you'd already have done so! In the last chapter you learned that asking for help is an excellent way to assist you in the recovery process. There are a variety of psychological treatments (known as *modalities*) that have been shown to help sufferers of C-PTSD that can be prescribed for you, and those are listed at the end of the chapter.

There are also exercises and techniques that you can learn to do yourself. In addition to working with a therapist, you can start counteracting the negative self-perception that you've been carrying around with you. There are known methods for helping you increase your self-esteem, as well as emotional regulation exercises. By working to grow as a person beyond the trauma, you open up whole new worlds for yourself and increase the possibility that you can find intimacy with others in a healthy, nourishing way.

Most of these exercises you'll need to revisit periodically, because one session isn't going to get you to where you want to go. You might feel that you're recovered to some extent, and then discover a new trigger or a new issue. Coming back and reusing these techniques will help you stay healthy and on your path.

There is hope. You don't have to suffer alone. Although right now you may feel completely isolated, there are others who have struggled just as you are. Not only are you not the only person to experience these issues, others have been able to heal from them. As they say, the journey of a thousand miles starts with one step. All you need is the willingness to take a step, and then take a step after that.

EXERCISES FOR BETTER SELF-PERCEPTION AND SELF-ESTEEM

You've learned how critical it is to look at yourself accurately, instead of through the dark lens that you've been using for so long. It may seem difficult, but you can prove to yourself that what you've been telling yourself up until now isn't actually true. In Chapter Five you learned about the mental habits that need to be adjusted in order for you to be more in tune with reality, and here are some activities to perform that will help you along the way.

Evidence that confirms or denies

In this exercise, you'll reflect on each belief that you have about yourself. On a sheet of paper or in a journal, divide the page into three columns. Label the left column "Proves" and the right column "Disproves."

In the middle, write down all the negative beliefs that you have about yourself and the negative self-talk. It might take you more than one session to identify them all, but at the end you want to make sure that you've written down every single one of them.

For each belief or negative statement, think of the evidence that you have that either proves or disproves what's in the middle column. Write them down in the appropriate column.

Suppose one of your beliefs is that you're always afraid. When you think about it, you remember a time in the past when you weren't afraid. You write that down in the right-hand column because it disproves this belief about yourself. Write down as much about this time you weren't afraid as you can recall. What was the situation, what action you took, how you felt, where you were, etc. If you can't remember all the details it's fine, but just write down as much as you can.

This not only helps you see that the belief is incorrect, but helps you remember what it was like not to be afraid. When you write it down, you can always look back on your evidence when the thought or belief comes back.

Repeat this for all your beliefs, and make sure that what you're writing down as evidence in either the Proves or Disproves column is true.

For example, suppose that you write down your belief that your date the previous night doesn't like you. You're tempted to write down the fact that they looked away from you while you were talking as proof. But is it really?

There are many reasons why they might have turned their head, and only one of them is because they don't like you. Unless they specifically said to you that they looked away because they don't like you, it's not proof of anything.

They said they'd like to see you again at the end of the date. Would someone who doesn't like you say that? You'd have to put that in the Disproves column.

Once you complete the exercise, if you've done it truthfully, you will probably have a lot more material in your Disproves column than in your Proves column. If that's not the case, I invite you to take a closer look at everything you considered proof. Is it really, or is it your negative thoughts tinting the facts?

You might have a couple of beliefs where you have more proof than disproof, or you might have none. If you have many though, you'll need to go back and think more objectively about the facts you have in evidence and see whether the proof really is true.

Reframe based on the previous exercise

Once you've finished the previous exercise, you'll see that you have disproved many of the negative statements you tell yourself. This shows you very clearly that what you think really isn't rooted in reality, because the facts are telling you something different.

Use this information to reframe your beliefs into something positive. When a negative statement or thought comes up, reframe it. Many people find it helpful to write down these new statements, so you have them handy when the old thoughts return.

For instance, in the example above you disproved the belief you had that your date's actions meant they didn't like you. You could reframe this in more than one positive way. You could say "Someone can look away from me when I'm speaking and still like me." Or "I don't always have to assume the worst about people." Or "I can look at the big picture and not worry about small circumstances like having a date look away from me."

You can do this for each belief. Suppose you proved to yourself that you're not always afraid, because you recalled times when you weren't afraid. You might say "I won't always be afraid," or "I may be afraid right now, but I won't always be."

It is important that you say things in a positive way but also be honest. If there's a statement that you're having difficulty with, you can always reframe it to something like, "I am working on [thing that's difficult]." For example, "I am working on not taking what other people do personally" or "I'm working on not being afraid all the time." Make sure it's both positive and true.

Over time you'll be able to do this exercise and have fewer negative beliefs, because the positive reframing you did helped require the pathways. And instead of saying "I'm working on not taking everything personally" you can truthfully say, "I don't have to take things personally" or even simply, "I don't take things personally."

Visualize achieving a goal or way you'd like to lead your life

Visualization is surprisingly powerful. When you're suffering from C-PTSD, in some ways your brain is (unintentionally) working against you. But when you can harness it in positive ways, it can help you more than you might think.

One thing that athletic coaches, especially at the elite competitive level, have known for some time is that visualizing the race or competition helps athletes win. For example, if you're a swimmer, your coach would advise you to make a movie in your mind where you feel yourself exploding off the starting block, quickly finding your rhythm, passing your closest competitor, and touching the wall first at the end.

When you visualize in detail, it's a dress rehearsal for what you're actually going to do. Your mind movie activates the same mental pathways that it does when you are actually performing the action (Swart, n.d.)[1]

You don't have to be an athlete to use visualization, as successful people in other areas of life do this as well. You can use it to work through a tricky situation that's coming up or think about how you would like your life to look in recovery, or to reach a certain goal.

For example, suppose you want to have a certain daily routine where you get out of bed, exercise (which is great for you for a variety of reasons), have a nutritious breakfast and some family time before you leave for work at a job that you love. Walk through this all in detail, including what it smells, sounds, tastes, and feels like, not just what it looks like. Feel (or imagine) how relaxed you are after a good night's sleep. Picture yourself putting on your favorite workout clothes that make you feel good.

What kind of exercise do you like? If it's biking, in your mind put on your helmet and start pedaling. If you're pedaling down a pretty forest path, imagine how good the woods smell and what the bird chirping sounds like. Or "hear" your favorite playlist.

Or maybe you prefer a hard mountain bike trail that's rough and rocky and gives you a thrill when you get to the top, just before you start blasting your way back down. Mentally see the obstacles you ride over and feel the wind in your face, the muscle tension in your arms and legs, the snapping of branches.

When your mind arrives back home, imagine sluicing off in the shower or bath and then putting on your favorite clothes for work. Then you get to sit down at the breakfast table with your family and your favorite thing to eat. Smell the eggs frying or the pancakes browning. Listen to the happy chatter of your kids and feel the dog's tail wagging against your leg.

Now you're on your commute to work. What music are you listening to? Where do you want to work—inside at the office, using the company truck to get around from site to site? Imagine a great day at work.

All that sensory detail is helpful for your brain. Many people like to make vision boards that keep these dreams or ideas front and center. You find images or objects that represent what you want and put them on the board where you're constantly reminded of them. You might cut out pictures from magazines or download them online; use objects that you've found, like stones that represent mountain biking; and anything that brings these details to mind.

There's a lot of stimuli out there in the world, so human brains naturally filter a lot of it out. Otherwise, there would be too much detail for the person to function. When you visualize and have a vision board, you're telling your brain what it should pay attention to.

Have you ever noticed that when you decide to buy a certain kind of car that all of a sudden you see that car everywhere you look? Suppose you decide you want to buy a Jeep or something like it for off-roading. All of a sudden, there are so many more Jeeps on the road than you've ever seen before!

It's not because everyone had the same idea as you, all at the same time. It's because you, in effect, told your brain to focus on Jeeps. Now your brain sees a Jeep and brings it to your attention. You just never noticed before because your brain was filtering them out instead.

Use this to your advantage. Tell it to pay attention to a job where you can drive around from site to site and make your own schedule because that's your preferred way of working. You can visualize your-self at such a job, and if you decide to use a vision board, find pictures of happy workers in their trucks. When your brain comes across something related to these images, it will stop filtering it out. You might catch a job listing or find someone who's working in a job like this, because your brain is now attuned to focusing on it.

Make three lists

In addition to reframing your negative beliefs about yourself, it's helpful to make positive lists. When you start off, you might find you don't have a whole lot of positive things to say. But keep adding to it. As you work on the healing process, you'll be able to set aside more negativity and discover more constructive ways to talk to yourself.

1. What you like about yourself

Everything you like needs to be on this list, no matter how silly you think it might be. Maybe, in addition to being kind to animals, you like that you can roll your tongue. Or you can imitate accents. Or you have compassion for others. Or you're good at playing with kids.

Whatever it is that's positive about you, write it down. Make sure you keep a copy of it so you can come back to it periodically. Refer to it when you're feeling particularly disappointed or upset with yourself, so you have a reminder of all your good qualities.

Also, reflect on it periodically through your healing journey. Many people start off feeling like they're weak but reach a point in the process where they're able to recognize how strong they really are, to have made it through. You can add it to the list. As you feel more secure and confident, you can try new things. You may or may not be a success. But you can still be proud of yourself for trying.

2. Your proudest moments in life

Likewise, when you reflect on your life you can find things that you did well or that reflect well on you. Maybe you found a dog lying by the side of the road and you took it to the vet. Making a friend who was having a hard day feel better. Write down as many as you can.

Reflect on this one too. Sometimes when you're feeling worthless or weak come back to the list and remind yourself that you have done worthy things and that you are a worthy person. And as you go through the process, come back to it to write down more things that you're proud of. You might have done things that you forgot about.

Or you've been doing activities during your healing that you can be proud of. Continue to add those to the list.

3. Everything you're thankful for

Take your time with this list. Write down as many as you possibly can, no matter how small it seems right now. Every tiny little thing counts. Once you've written them all down, cut the sheet of paper into strips with one item of gratitude on the strip. Fold them up and put them in a jar or other container.

When you could use a shot of gratitude - which is usually when you're feeling bad - dip into the jar and grab a piece of paper at random. Read your statement. If you need more, pull out more. When you're able to shift into a feeling of gratitude, refold them and put them back in the jar so they're available for next time.

Any time you think of something else to be grateful for, write it down and put it in the jar. Like the other two lists, these will probably grow as you progress along your road to recovery.

It's important to remember that the road isn't usually linear. Most people don't go from suffering C-PTSD symptoms to being recovered in a completely straight line. Instead, for many you make some progress, and then either plateau or retreat a little bit. Then you move forward again, and again there will be a hiccup.

If you move back one step for every two steps forward, you're still making progress. Don't let the interruptions, plateaus, and bumps throw you. They'll happen, but you can keep moving forward anyway.

Help another person

If you've ever been in a 12-step recovery program, you might be familiar with the saying, "If you want self-esteem, perform esteemable acts." Helping other people isn't the only method of creating a truer self-perception that isn't so negative, but it is a good one.

And it doesn't have to be big: you don't have to save someone's life or donate a kidney. You could let someone who's got two small children and a big shopping cart and look of exhaustion go ahead of you in line at the grocery store. You could pay for the person behind you at the coffee shop.

Pick up whatever the person in front of you dropped, particularly if they're elderly or otherwise have a hard time bending down. Give up your seat on the bus to someone who's older or more tired than you. Small acts of helping may be the only things you can do for others at the moment, and they're still good for the person you're helping as well as yourself.

This works in two ways for you, the helper. One is that you get that release of the Happiness Trifecta neurochemicals, so you get pleasure out of the deal. It also helps you affirm to yourself that you are a good, giving person. That you're not as bad as you sometimes tell yourself that you are. The more you help, the better you'll feel about yourself.

And sometimes it's just nice to get out of your own head. Even people without a disorder of some kind like to spend time concentrating on other people so they don't have to think about themselves or worry about anything. They can focus on the other person instead.

Practice self-confident body language

As you become better able to recognize your own positive traits and be less negative in your self-talk, you'll be more confident. Another powerful way to boost your self-confidence is to act like it.

While in many aspects of life it's not possible to "fake it 'til you make it," self-confidence is an outlier in this regard. To some extent, the more you practice acting self-confident, the more self-assured you'll feel. That doesn't mean that you can do a "power pose" for a couple of minutes and suddenly you're ready to take on the world! But it does mean that you can act *as if* you're self-confident and it will have a positive impact.

Earlier in the book we discussed the mind-body connection, and that it goes both ways, not just from mind to body. Smiling even when you don't feel like it tells your brain that you're happy, or at least pleased about something. Even a fake smile can change your mood.

Similarly, taking on self-confident body language tells your mind that you are feeling self-confident. Regularly doing so can help you strengthen that positive pathway in your brain. The good news is that acting as if you're self-confident isn't really all that hard. You don't have to do any strange contortions or stand on one leg or anything physically difficult.

When you think about confidence, who springs to mind? An athlete like Serena Williams or Lionel Messi? Or maybe you're thinking of business leaders, such as Richard Branson or Jeff Bezos. Perhaps you've got a politician in mind, or a friend you know who always seems self-assured.

How do they stand? When they talk to reporters, how do they hold themselves, and where are they looking? When they enter a room, what do they do when they want to introduce themselves to someone? How do they walk around the room?

You can probably picture a lot of that in your head right now. They stand tall with their heads held high. When they speak to people, even reporters, they look directly into the other person's eyes. They smile and nod at what the other person's saying - sometimes even when the reporter's giving them a hard time!

When a confident person walks into a room, they have that same erect stance, and when they see someone they want to talk to, they introduce themselves and give a firm handshake. As they're walking around the room, they plant their feet firmly and move without much hesitation.

Even if you're not feeling particularly (or even at all) confident in yourself, you can still mimic these mannerisms and they'll help you feel more positive. Best of all, you can practice many of these moves wherever you are.

Stand tall when you're in line at the grocery store. Look directly at the cashier when you're ordering food. Not only does the eye contact benefit you, but it helps them feel like less of a robot. Win-win! People respond well to others who appear confident, so you may find that your interactions improve while you're practicing.

With your friends you can practice standing tall and shaking hands, in addition to eye contact and allowing yourself to react to their speech with nods and smiles. Even when you're watching TV at home, practice sitting tall with your head held high and shoulders back instead of hunched or curved.

There are ways to stand to give yourself a temporary confidence boost as well. A well-known "power pose" is to stand tall with your legs spread apart and hands on your hips. This appears aggressive to other people if you do it in front of them, so try to do it when no one's watching. Or in a quiet place just before you do something that triggers anxiety, like a job interview or speaking on stage.

There's a lot of information available elsewhere about body language, but the basics of confidence will help you on your journey to recovery.

Make positive and truthful affirmations

Affirmations, while they may sound a little weird or silly, do have neuroscience backing their use. The more you repeat positive affirmations, the more those constructive neural pathways get strengthened while you sleep.

It's also important that you believe what you're saying. For example, if you're unhappy with your body because it's too thin, you won't believe yourself if you say something like, "My body is the right weight." That type of affirmation doesn't help. Instead, you can change it to something that is true, such as "I am working on my body to achieve a weight I am happy with" or a similar statement.

Affirmations will also work much better if you genuinely think about what you're saying as you make the statements. If you just blast through them without thinking, you're not giving your brain a lot of time to process and really be aware of what you want it to pay attention to. Really think about what each statement means as you say it.

You can give yourself reminders, such as putting them on sticky notes on your mirror or in your phone with an alarm so that you do your affirmations every day. Once daily is good, but twice is even better.

If you're not sure what affirmations to use, you can try this exercise of seven sets, memorizing one per week. After you've practiced consistently for seven weeks, you'll have a healthier view of yourself.

Week one

1. I accept responsibility for myself and for everything I think, say, and do.
2. I choose to stay constructive in my actions.
3. I refuse to talk negatively to and about myself and to accept the negativity others may have towards me.
4. I make choices and accept the results of those choices.
5. I control the expression of my thoughts, ideas, wants, expectations, and perceptions.

Week two

1. I do my own thinking and act accordingly.
2. When I make a mistake or experience defeats or losses, I don't blame anyone else.
3. I enjoy doing my work to the best of my ability and on a consistent basis.
4. I do not attach to thoughts of shame, guilt, or blame.

Week three

1. I accept that problems and obstacles are challenges for my own personal development.
2. I rid myself of shame, guilt, or blame.
3. I don't procrastinate because my goals motivate me.
4. I don't quit.
5. I don't compare myself to anyone else, nor do I let comparisons affect me.

Week four

1. I do my best to develop and maintain a positive image of myself.
2. I am always authentic and true to myself.
3. I don't base who I am on what roles I play in life.
4. I totally and unconditionally accept myself exactly the way I am.

Week five

1. I am confident in my convictions and stand up for them.
2. I rely on myself for support, both financially and morally.
3. I see reality clearly and let go the things I can't change.
4. I don't allow fear of failure or rejection to hold me back.

Week six

1. I don't need anyone else's approval for the way I live my life.
2. I don't let others talk me into things that aren't good for me.
3. I treat myself gently and kindly.
4. I don't overdo it, preferring to avoid excess.

Week seven

1. I stand tall and smile when I greet others.
2. My mistakes teach me lessons I learn.
3. I don't need to impress others with my importance or value.
4. I love being me.

SELF-CARE AS BEST YOU CAN

You've probably had well-meaning people tell you about these acts of self-care in the belief that they would "fix" you. They won't, but they can help you in your quest for trauma recovery. These are ways that you can be kind and compassionate to yourself, as well as giving you the best chance for healing. These are good habits that will help you with physical health, which also supports your mental health.

Sleep

Any form of PTSD, including Complex, usually results in sleep difficulties. But the more you can practice what's known as "good sleep hygiene," the better off you'll be along your journey to recovery.

Standard go to sleep/wake up times

Since sleep for many survivors isn't very deep or healing, they often find themselves sleeping in the morning or during the day. This makes it hard to sleep at night and creates a vicious cycle. Try to stick to a schedule for the entire week and not alter it too much.

If you wake up very tired, you can have a quick nap in the late morning or early afternoon. Keep it quick and early so you can get through the day without compromising your nighttime sleep.

No screens, heavy exercise, heavy food, or heavy alcohol within an hour of bedtime

Modern screens, which means cellphones, tablets, laptops, TVs, etc., emit blue light which tricks your body into thinking it's daylight, so it doesn't release the sleep prep mechanism (melatonin). Give your body a break so it can get ready for sleep naturally.

Heavy food, exercise, and drink within an hour of sleep will prevent you from having the rest that you need. You'll likely be waking up frequently even if you can get to sleep easily.

What can you do in that hour? Spend time with the family, on a favorite hobby, reading, or any combination of these three.

Keep your cell phone in another room

In addition to the blue light the screen emits, most people have notifications and messages beeping and buzzing and flashing lights. These are bad for everyone, not just people with C-PTSD. Keep your phone charger in a different room and leave your phone there overnight.

There's no reason for you to wake up and immediately scroll through social media or check your email. Give yourself time in the morning to do positive things like exercise, meditate, and repeat your affirmations.

Keep the room quiet, dark, and cool

Most people sleep best when their environment is dark, not too warm, and silent. There are a variety of ways that you can achieve all these objectives, according to what you personally find comfortable.

You can buy eye masks, most of which can also be heated up or cooled depending on preference. Some come with soothing scents like lavender. Or you can get room-darkening shades to block out light for the whole room (or both).

Earplugs or sound generators are great ways to shut out noise. Turn down your thermostat in the winter for better sleeping and use a ceiling or other fan in the summer to keep the room cool.

Nutritious food

You don't have to follow a specific diet if you don't want to. You probably already know what's good for you to eat: a balance of fruits and vegetables, lean protein, good fats like avocados, walnuts, olives and their oils, and whole grains. Not too much.

Processed food has a lot of preservatives as well as sugar, fat, and salt which can damage your body. Think of adding healthy, pretty food with vibrant colors like berries instead of what you're removing from your diet (store cookies, fried foods, too much fast food.)

Exercise

It's not so much about what you do as making sure you're consistently doing it. If you haven't been moving at all, make it a goal to walk outside for ten minutes a day to start and work your way up. The guidelines recommend 150 minutes moderate exercise per week for basic health.

It's best not to do one 150-minute session or two 75-minute ones, but to do something more like half an hour five days a week. Brisk walking counts as moderate exercise, so if you can get out the door for half an hour a day and walk briskly, you're all set. Bring the family with you too!

If you really don't think you have a half hour all at once in your day, don't worry, you can break that up into two 15-minute sessions or three 10-minute sessions. And if you don't like walking, do what you like, as long as it's moderate (or harder). Play tennis or basketball, dance, and mix things up so you don't get bored.

Hydration

The body is on average mostly water (60%) and your brain is composed of even more water, about 73%. When you're not getting enough water, your body isn't working optimally. Food that is mostly water, like strawberries and watermelon, counts toward your intake.

Get a reusable water bottle and bring it with you. You can find some that tell you how much to fill up each day and how much you should drink by a certain time if you find that helpful. Reusable water bottles cause less environmental harm than water you pick up in bottles at the store. Start drinking! If you live in a dry climate or at high altitude you may find you need more water.

Mindfulness exercises

Earlier in this book we mentioned that meditation is a good way to get started with mindfulness, and that guided meditations are good for beginners. You can choose any method that works for you. Mindfulness is one of the best ways to develop better emotional regulation (The Wellness Society, n.d.)[2]

Some people don't do well with traditional meditation and that's OK. Exercise itself can be a good way to be mindful. Or you can choose an activity during the day to really experience, like brushing your teeth, washing dishes, or taking a shower.

Key into the sounds, smells, and how it feels in and on your body for the short time that you do these activities. Pay attention only to what you're doing, and when your mind wanders (as it likely will) just bring yourself gently back to the activity.

It's also helpful to combine mindfulness, breathing, and movement. Becoming aware of your body and your breathing sensations helps you feel safe with your body. Instead of being fearful of it, you can learn to approach with curiosity instead. As strange as this may sound, you can actually practice and get better at relaxing.

There are a variety of methods you can try. Some you've probably heard of and others you might not have, but you can find information about all of these online. You might be able to find a teacher of the practice near you, and if not, you can search for online classes.

Yoga

There are many varieties of yoga, and you'll likely find a studio or classes near you. It is common for yoga instructors to touch students to help guide them into the poses or movements correctly. If that's an issue, you can let the instructor know ahead of time. Or stream classes in your home.

The Wellness Society notes that the ending pose for most yoga classes, known as Shavasana, is particularly helpful for helping you learn to relax. In this pose you simply lie on your back with limbs relaxed and eyes closed for a period of time, usually several minutes.

Tae Kwan Do (or Taekwondo)

This Korean martial art is about much more than fighting. If you've seen competitions, you've seen some amazing kicks, as the name is about the discipline of "fists and feet." However, the other element is discipline.

Taekwondo practices unity: body, mind, and life, and dealing with confrontation (USATKD, n.d.)[3] Its practitioners seek harmonious personal development.

Tai Chi (tai chi chuan)

Originally, the Chinese practiced this as a martial art, but now it's used as a form of exercise that employs grace in its movements. Each action flows naturally and smoothly into the next and is accompanied by deep breathing. It's noncompetitive, and like yoga, there's more than one style.

It's low impact and suitable for most people, including older adults.

Qi Gong (chi kung)

This Asian practice is similar to yoga, with many different styles. It also incorporates breathing, posture, and movement. The name refers to skill obtained by practice and breath or energy.

Feldenkrais

This is a method that uses visualization and gentle movement to focus on functionality. It too makes use of awareness (connecting the physical body to what's going on within you) and breathing techniques. The Russian doctor Moshe Feldenkrais developed it to help people live the life they want.

Quit smoking, and quit drinking

There are no health benefits to smoking, and a variety of methods of quitting. If you know cold turkey won't work for you, try using a patch or gum or other way that you can gradually decrease your use.

Even one drink per day has been proven to have a negative impact on health mentally and physically. Any benefits in alcoholic drinks can be found in other substitutes. For example, the antioxidant *resveratrol* is the healthy element in a glass of wine, but you can also get it by eating skin-on red grapes.

PSYCHOLOGICAL TREATMENTS

In addition to the suggestions and exercises above that you can do yourself or practice with friends, loved ones, and/or fellow survivors, there are a number of therapeutic treatments that have been shown to help C-PTSD sufferers begin to live a better life.

Unfortunately, our culture tends to stigmatize people with mental health issues. We don't try to shame someone with a broken foot for getting treatment, and likewise no one who has a mental health condition should be shamed for it either. But people do. However, don't let this hold you back from seeking help.

As noted earlier, the disorder is called "Complex" for a reason. It's not like having the flu, or a broken leg, or even something as relatively "simple" as depression with no other conditions. People don't simply grow out of it. Or get better by eating nutritious food and getting enough sleep, though those things are certainly helpful. There are a variety of symptoms that require treatment in order to heal.

Because of the nature of complex trauma, it's not very likely that you'll be able to heal yourself without some competent therapeutic help. Don't be shy about seeking it out. You'll want to find someone who specializes in C-PTSD (or DESNOS), if you can; otherwise, an expert in PTSD is best.

Finding one is fortunately not as hard as it used to be with the internet, and you can make your search in private if you're concerned about anyone finding out. If you're a veteran, whether or not your complex trauma resulted from your service, check with the Veterans

Administration and their mental health resources. Fortunately, they have a lot of expertise in helping people recover from PTSD and C-PTSD.

If you work for a large company, they may have an EAP or Employee Assistance Program that can help refer you to someone who'll be able to help you. It's possible they'll have someone on staff who's an expert, but more likely they'll help you find someone. You can also search the Internet for therapists and doctors who specialize in C-PTSD and see if you can find one near you. If you're in the US and mental health isn't covered by your insurance, many have sliding scale fees where you pay what you can afford.

Anxiety can be either mentally or physically based. A treatment that's based on reframing your thoughts may not work as well when your anxiety has become so physical that now fear itself is the problem. Once you find someone to help you, they may work with one or more of the following *modalities* or types of treatment.

Cognitive behavioral therapy (CBT)

This method is used with a variety of disorders including anxiety and depression. It involves looking at your thoughts to see if they're true. You learn to stop attaching to your thoughts and to reframe back to reality when negativity strikes. This can be very effective for mental anxiety but may not work as well for anyone who's dealing with the physical type.

Although you do talk about your thoughts with your therapist, you're not typically lying down on a couch and closing your eyes as you might have seen on TV or in the movies. Normally you'll both be sitting across from each other and having more of a conversation.

EMDR

Eye Movement Desensitization and Reprocessing seems to make disturbing thoughts less intense by using eye movement (typically side to side). The eye movements are similar to what our eyes do in REM sleep, which is when we dream and find associations between memories.

Similarly, EMDR can help people get more perspective on their trauma, by moving it to regular memory and relegating it to something that happened in the past instead of now.

Sensorimotor psychotherapy

This modality focuses on the body and what we can learn from physical reactions, so it can be worthwhile for those suffering from physical anxiety. It works with the body as well as the thinking mind and emotions. (Sensorimotor refers to pathways that involve sensory and motor functions, which basically means body movements.)

Pesso-Boyden System Psychomotor (PBSP)

Developed by two dancers, PBSP combines a body and mind approach. You learn exercises that help you learn about your sensorimotor and emotional signals in your own unique body.

Somatic experiencing

Another body-oriented therapy, it helps you make use of your body's own healing systems. While you're tracking feelings, images, and sensations in your body, you'll learn how to get past the emotionally frozen state of overwhelm.

The Comprehensive Resource Model (CRM)

Instead of a phased model, in CRM the work occurs simultaneously. The therapist helps you find that everything you need is within you and teaches you how to ultimately do this on your own.

Internal Family Systems (IFS)

IFS may sound like "family therapy," which many addicts are exposed to in a treatment center, but it's actually quite different. Many people feel that they're made up of different parts and each part has a different role. For example, you might have a version of you as a frightened child, a boss or thinker, someone who gets angry very easily, a people-pleaser, and so on. This therapy helps you integrate all your different parts, because there's a reason each of them is there. You don't need to get rid of any of them, and all of them can work towards your healing.

Tension, Stress and Trauma Release (TRE)

Developed by a doctor who noticed that children in bomb shelters shake like animals when they're scared but adults don't, this method takes the natural inclination to shake as a way to recover. Shaking, or vibrating if you prefer, soothes muscle tension and the nervous system as a whole (The Wellness Society, n.d.)[4]

However, a word of caution here: C-PTSD patients may feel retraumatized if they do too much too soon. Start with a minute or two, two or three times a week. Or better yet, find a certified practitioner by searching online.

If the first therapist that you see doesn't make you feel safe or comfortable with them after a few sessions (it may take you a while to trust them), feel free to search for another. And if a modality isn't working for you after several months and you don't see progress, you can discuss your expectations with the therapist. It does take time, so don't expect to be healed in a few sessions.

If you don't want to tell anyone because you're afraid of the stigma, that's OK. Just don't stop going or doing whatever "homework" your therapist may recommend. Your healing is the most important thing, not what anyone else thinks or says about it.

CHAPTER SUMMARY

While it's not the easiest journey, it is possible for a complex trauma survivor to regain control over their lives and begin to live the way that they prefer, without constant hyperarousal and fear around triggers.

- There are exercises that you can do to improve your self-perception and self-esteem, including positive affirmations, acting in a self-confident way even when you don't feel like

it, and making lists of the things that you like about yourself
and have accomplished that you can refer to regularly.

- Practicing self-care in the form of getting enough sleep,
  eating well, staying hydrated, exercising, etc. won't heal you,
  but they will make it easier for you on your journey to
  recovery.

- Complex trauma often requires the help of a therapist to
  unlock healing, and there are several therapeutic techniques
  they may use including cognitive behavior therapy, EMDR,
  and internal family systems.

FINAL WORDS

While Complex Post-Traumatic Stress Disorder is not as well-known as PTSD itself, it has a significant impact on its sufferers. Survivors of complex trauma can go through the recovery process and begin to function more normally. However, they have to address the problem because it won't heal on its own or go away after a period of time.

There are a lot of situations in this book that you might relate to and lots of information, so don't worry if you feel a bit like you're drinking from a firehose. You can always go back and refresh yourself on the topics when questions come up. Healing from complex trauma isn't usually a linear process, where you start at one end and make steady gains every day or week until you reach functionality. You might make big gains and then end up walking them back a bit, before you make another leap.

First you discovered what trauma is: an event that affects the nervous system and prevents it from functioning properly. The brain essentially gets stuck in the fear response and can't return to normal. People respond to trauma in common ways, and PTSD won't be diagnosed unless the person has been suffering the same symptoms for over a month since the incident.

They must be re-experiencing the traumatic event, often as nightmares or flashbacks, and trying to avoid any reminders or triggers of the event, often going out of their way to do so. In addition, the person must be feeling like they're constantly under threat, which can be expressed through an excessive startle response or being constantly on edge.

Usually, trauma happens once and for a discrete period of time. For example, a car crash, a mugging, a sexual assault are all traumas that can lead to PTSD. However, the Complex form is characterized by repeated traumas over a period of time. For example, childhood abuse, domestic abuse, being a refugee, and living in a war-torn or otherwise violent and chaotic environment.

While the World Health Organization classifies it as a separate mental health condition, the US diagnostic tool known as the DSM-V considers it a DESNOS diagnosis - Disorders of Extreme Stress Not Otherwise Specified. As well as the regular PTSD symptoms, someone with the Complex form experiences *affect dysregulation*, or the inability to manage and control their emotions. They also have an extremely negative self-perception and have intense difficulties in their relationships with others.

C-PTSD shows up in people in a variety of ways, including physical symptoms such as pain, digestive disorders. People with the disorder often believe that they're alone in their misery and have feelings of guilt and shame. It's common for additional *comorbid* conditions like substance or sexual addiction to be present as well.

You also learned that the disorder stems from brain processes that have gone awry as a result of the trauma. Ordinarily, when the fight-or-flight reflex is activated, the person's systems return to baseline and the fear response is no longer activated. However, with complex trauma the brain doesn't receive the instructions to "stand down" and continues on as if the person is in immediate physical danger. It's not known yet what exactly causes C-PTSD in some people and not in others with similar experiences, but there are some underlying conditions that make the diagnosis more likely. Mood and personality disorders, anxious temperaments, and lifestyle factors like a lack of support may all contribute.

The book covered the specific symptoms of C-PTSD in detail, including affect dysregulation, avoidance, disturbance in interpersonal relationships, re-experiencing the trauma, and negative self-perception. Finally, in the last chapter you discovered suggestions and steps that you can take to help overcome the negative self-perception and take better care of yourself, as well as a summary of the psychological tools that a therapist can provide.

The most important thing I want you to take from this book is that you are worthy of recovering and that you can do it, as long as you tackle it. As someone who's been affected by C-PTSD, I know what it's like to feel shame about what happened and to be down on yourself for your supposed weakness. I say "supposed" because it takes a lot of strength to survive and keep going!

Even if you're not sure you're worth it right now, try to start your healing journey. It is possible, and you'll eventually get to the point where you can feel worthy of recovery. C-PTSD touches everyone in your life, not just you, and recovery benefits them as well. But primarily it's your journey, and you're the one who will heal and develop so that you can lead the life you want.

You've now got the tools from this book, and you can also seek out help to support you. Take action now so that you can have a life that doesn't revolve around avoiding triggers or upsetting emotional outbursts. Don't close this book and leave it on your shelf, digital or otherwise. Use what's in here to start and stay motivated as you make your way to recovery.

I want to make sure that everyone who could use this book knows it's here for them. If you found this book helpful, please leave a review on Amazon so that it can reach others.

NOTES

INTRODUCTION

1. https://www.therecoveryvillage.com/mental-health/ptsd/related/ptsd-statistics/

1. WHAT IS COMPLEX TRAUMA?

1. https://www.dictionary.com/browse/trauma?s=t
2. https://www.verywellmind.com/common-symptoms-after-a-traumatic-event-2797496
3. https://www.researchgate.net/publication/12554195_Posttraumatic_stress_disorder_The_burden_to_the_individual_and_to_society
4. https://apps.who.int/iris/bitstream/handle/10665/85623/9789241505932_eng.pdf;jsessionid=23D482DC7C709E883922871E785F4161?sequence=1
5. https://www.psychologytoday.com/us/blog/fostering-freedom/202005/revictimization-how-can-keep-happening

2. WHERE DOES C-PTSD COME FROM?

1. https://www.verywellmind.com/what-is-the-fight-or-flight-response-2795194
2. https://bigthink.com/experts-corner/decisions-are-emotional-not-logical-the-neuroscience-behind-decision-making
3. https://www.psychologytoday.com/us/blog/in-the-body/201910/when-trauma-gets-stuck-in-the-body
4. https://www.ncbi.nlm.nih.gov/pmc/articles/PMC2816923/
5. https://www.ncbi.nlm.nih.gov/pmc/articles/PMC4263906/
6. Ibid.
7. https://www.ncbi.nlm.nih.gov/pmc/articles/PMC3614697/
8. Ibid.
9. https://eating-disorders.org.uk/information/why-people-get-eating-disorders/

10. https://www.verywellmind.com/ptsd-causes-and-risk-factors-2797397

3. SYMPTOMS OF PTSD

1. https://www.talkspace.com/blog/happens-brain-ptsd-flashback-2/
2. https://www.ptsd.va.gov/understand/related/nightmares.asp
3. https://www.psychologytoday.com/us/blog/the-aftermath-trauma/201407/what-dreams-may-come-treating-the-nightmares-ptsd
4. https://www.whoop.com/thelocker/stages-of-sleep-cycles/
5. https://www.sciencedaily.com/releases/2017/11/171103085308.htm
6. https://www.bbc.com/future/article/20140728-why-is-all-the-news-bad
7. https://depts.washington.edu/psyclerk/glossary.html
8. https://www.militarytimes.com/pay-benefits/military-benefits/health-care/2015/03/30/depression-or-ptsd-can-cause-irritability/
9. https://www.verywellmind.com/sleep-problems-when-you-have-ptsd-2797478
10. CRF: corticotropin-releasing factor

4. AFFECT DYSREGULATION

1. https://psychcentral.com/blog/what-is-affect-or-emotion-dysregulation
2. https://traumaticstressinstitute.org/wp-content/files_mf/1276631745ShameandAttachment.pdf
3. https://www.nationaleatingdisorders.org/blog/eating-disorders-and-complex-post-traumatic-stress-disorder
4. https://www.ncbi.nlm.nih.gov/pmc/articles/PMC5902809/
5. https://www.goodtherapy.org/learn-about-therapy/issues/aggression-violence

5. NEGATIVE SELF-CONCEPT

1. https://www.simplypsychology.org/self-concept.html
2. Ibid.

6. DISTURBED INTERPERSONAL RELATIONSHIPS

1. https://www.psychologytoday.com/us/blog/vitality/201404/the-neuroscience-giving
2. https://www.simplypsychology.org/maslow.html
3. https://psychcentral.com/lib/c-ptsd-and-interpersonal-relationships
4. https://www.goodtherapy.org/blog/psychpedia/intimacy
5. https://www.brightquest.com/blog/complex-ptsd-and-romantic-relationships-healing-trauma-together-through-treatment/

7. RECOVERING AND RECLAIMING YOUR IDENTITY

1. https://www.fastcompany.com/90346545/this-is-a-visualization-exercise-that-actually-works-according-to-neuroscience
2. https://thewellnesssociety.org/healing-cptsd-the-ultimate-online-guide/
3. https://www.teamusa.org/usa-taekwondo/v2-getting-started-in-taekwondo/what-is-taekwondo
4. https://thewellnesssociety.org/healing-cptsd-the-ultimate-online-guide/

Printed in Great Britain
by Amazon

87414598R00123